Uncertainty & Plenitude

Peter Stitt

Uncertainty
&Plenitude
FIVE CONTEMPORARY POETS

UNIVERSITY OF IOWA PRESS ᴪ Iowa City

University of Iowa Press,

Iowa City 52242

Copyright © 1997 by the

University of Iowa Press

All rights reserved

Printed in the United States

of America

Design by Richard Hendel

http://www.uiowa.edu/~uipress

Printed on acid-free paper

Library of Congress
Cataloging-in-Publication Data

Stitt, Peter.

Uncertainty and plenitude: five contemporary
poets / by Peter Stitt.

p.   cm.

Includes bibliographical references and index.

ISBN 0-87745-599-6

1. American poetry—20th century—History
and criticism.   2. Ashbery, John—Criticism
and interpretation.   3. Dobyns, Stephen, 1941–
—Criticism and interpretation.   4. Simic,
Charles, 1938–   —Criticism and interpretation.
5. Stern, Gerald, 1925–   —Criticism and
interpretation.   6. Wright, Charles, 1935–
—Criticism and interpretation.   I. Title.

PS325.S85   1997

811'5409—dc21   97-8756

02   01   00   99   98   97   C   5   4   3   2   1

JEAN STRAUB STITT

Mia Secchia, La Squisita

She is the eye of the grove, the eye of mimosa and willow.

The cypress behind her catches fire.

—James Wright

Contents

Introduction

Poetry in a Time of Uncertainty and Plenitude

We live in an age of plenitude, an age of muchness, the muchness age, and that means poetry, too. But some people who love poetry love also to bewail its tiny status, its lack of money and fame, its permanent position in America's backseat, rumble seat, potty chair; poetry seems all but obliterated in our culture, seems mummified and miniaturized beside so many lively and important things, things of which there is so much — so much TV, so much rock and roll, so much news, so much Mozart; so many sports, so many games, so many contests on TV; so much style, so many clothes and earrings and nose-rings and pierced eyebrows; so much purple hair, so many redheads, henna-heads, blonde-and-hennaheads, skinheads, ponytailheads, ponytail-emerging-from-buzzcutheads; so many movies, so many films, so much cinematography; so many people, so much population problem; so many novels, so much fiction, so many exposés, so many true stories, true confessions, false confessions; so many serial murderers, so many loaded guns, so much random killing, so much crack cocaine, so many drug dealers; so much terror, so much doubt, so much uncertainty; so much death of God, so much fundamentalism, so many TV preachers, so many infomercials, so many one-day seminars, so much team building, so many hucksters, critics, theorists; so much real world, so many trees and shrubs and squirrels and mourning doves, so many varieties of azaleas, so many beautiful cars, so much automotive splendor, so many drivers, so many readers, so many writers and poets, so much art, so much poetry, so much contemporary poetry.

No one book could comprehend it all, and this one does not intend to: although I have chosen to write only about poets whose work I admire, I am by no means going to write about all of those. There are far too many for discussion in one book, just as there are too many poets whose work I do not like, and too many whose work leaves me numb with indifference. From within this great plenitude, I have chosen to write about five poets — John Ashbery, Stephen Dobyns, Charles Simic, Gerald Stern, and Charles Wright — or six, if I count Stanley Kunitz, whose poetry I discuss briefly with that of Wright. I choose these particular writers because their work continues to interest me deeply, both intellectually and formally, even after years of familiarity with it.

In each of the five essays, I intend to give — from my own, inevitably subjective, perspective — a full discussion of the formal and intellectual aspects of the work of one of these poets, using what I believe are representative poems. I have no desire to discuss all of the work of any of them; indeed, I will not even discuss all of the individual books written by any of them. Rather, I will discuss those poems that I find definitive of each poet's vision and achievement, poems that are representative. If I have chosen wisely, then the points I make about these poems will apply as well to other poems by the same writer. I will pay attention to chronology and generally discuss poems from all phases of each writer's career. I may discuss them as significant individual pieces or as parts of a cohesive larger unit, such as the particular book within which they appear; I will occasionally choose not to discuss whole groups of poems, or even entire books of poems, when I find them off the major track of the poet, or of subpar quality. By the end of each essay, I hope that I will have given a full account of what I consider to be each poet's major track.

It is essential to choose, just as it is essential to know that one is choosing. It is essential to know that in choosing to take one path, you are choosing not to take an infinite number of other paths, and that you repeat this process with every step you take. It is essential to know that each of those other paths is still there, even though you did not choose it. It is essential to know that each of those other paths may be just as valid as the one you did choose. In an age of plenitude, an age of uncertainty, you may be certain of these things only: that the path you chose did not exist until you chose it; that it is your path and yours alone; that there is no one path, no right path, no wrong path, not even for you alone; that your path has no ultimate value, your destination no ultimate meaning; that you have no idea of your destination.

Poems are works of art, and this means that — within the nature of their being — form is at least as important as content. Thus I mean to be talking about form, either implicitly or explicitly, whenever I am discussing poems in my essays. Sometimes, however, the role of form here will be so implicit — so deeply hidden — within a consideration of content that some readers may think it is not present at all. I believe, however, that if one is truly discussing the content of the poem, rather than merely discussing the subject matter that the poem also happens to discuss, then one is inevitably discussing form: in a work of art, the two cannot be separated. I agree with Archibald MacLeish that "A poem should be equal to: / Not true." I agree also with a distinction on the subject of form once made by John Berryman. The poet Madeline DeFrees — when she was still known as Sister Mary Gilbert — spent an important summer studying the craft of poetry under Berryman's tutelage at the University of Indiana. Berryman, she says, preferred to divide the formal elements of poetry into two components: those that work on the surface of the poem, and those that work at a deeper level, where form intersects with meaning.[1]

Berryman used the term "surface form" to refer to the aesthetic elements of the poem: sound devices — such as rhythm, meter, rhyme, assonance, consonance, alliteration — and visual devices — such as descriptive and ornamental imagery. These elements determine the beauty of the poem, its aural and visual attractiveness; they are primarily what makes it a work of art. However, the conceptual significance of a poem — which should have its own degree of aesthetic beauty — is primarily expressed not through these relatively ornamental devices but through the more substantial elements that Berryman grouped under the heading of "deep form," the elements that determine intellectual structure and meaning — for example: syntax, tone, voice; character, incident, setting; the juxtaposition of detail; meaning-bearing imagery, including metaphor and simile; and other things.

Before it has meaning, poetry is art; it intends to give us aesthetic pleasure. I, too, studied with John Berryman, in a full-year course called "The European

Heritage" at the University of Minnesota, and I remember him reading Dante aloud, in medieval Italian, so we would appreciate the sound, the beauty, the art of the poetry, and not worry yet about its meanings.[2] Before its content is revealed to the reader, a poem is pure art; before it achieves meaning, a poem has music, incident, description. But poetry is still art after we know its meaning; it still intends to give us aesthetic pleasure. Perhaps the greatest error endemic to contemporary literary criticism is the assumption that aesthetics has nothing to do with truth, beauty nothing to do with meaning.

The academic critics that we often too casually lump together as deconstructionists are particularly prone to this error; their theoretic emphasis on semantics and on the social implications of literary discourse causes them to ignore aesthetics almost entirely. Other thinkers, however, more rigorous thinkers — philosophers and theoretical physicists prominently among them — have always recognized that an important test of any intellectual construct is the beauty of its formulation. This is why the precise exercise of logic is as graceful as ballet, why a solid mathematical proof is as elegant and beautiful as a symphony. Simplicity, elegance, beauty, grace — these are hallmarks of both good thinking and good making.

Thus it is because I believe that form is essential to a full appreciation and understanding of poetry that I wish it always to be present in my discussions of these poems. Somewhere in each of my essays I will attempt to describe, define, and evaluate the surface strategies of the poet; occasionally I will even try to relate these elements to the meaning of the poems. Generally, however, I agree with John Berryman in thinking that surface form does not have much to do with content; and I am seriously interested in content. Thus most of my analysis of form will either be explicitly present as I discuss the general rhetorical strategies of the poems, or implicitly present as I discuss the content — meaning the *nature* of the content — of the poems. Readers conditioned to believe that surface form is the only kind of form may think that I am not interested in form, but only in content. My goal, however, is always to be discussing form, and I hope that my discussions of meaning will never wander entirely away from this core concern. As I discuss these poets, I wish to explain not only what they are about, what they are saying, but how they are about it, how they say it.

Given the fundamental importance that I assign to matters of form, I feel it is essential that I preserve as much as possible of the full effect, aesthetic and intellectual, of the poems that I discuss. Thus I will present them generously; I will quote from them liberally and I will often paraphrase the parts of a poem that I do not quote. Though some readers may be impatient with this method, I trust that most will appreciate the opportunity to savor, or resavor, the fullness of these poems. Nearly everything I have to say is based on the poetic texts; there are no abstract theories, disconnected from the tangible, in my essays.

I believe that the thesis of this book is to do what I have described, to enact that process. I am not a literary theorist; my ambition is to add lumination to the poetic texts, not to use them as the basis for my own abstract speculations. On those occasions when I do seem to wander away from the texts in order to offer a profundity of my own, I hope that my readers will accept what I have to say as a bonus, a quantum of muchness, the sort of thing that you get when you cash in frequent-flyer miles. I do not, however, intend to offer an all-encompassing theory of contemporary American poetry. As I have already indicated, when I look at the universe of contemporary American poetry, I see a plenitude of thematic concerns and artistic approaches; I do not see an undeniable oneness, an overriding principle of cohesion linking large numbers of writers together. And yet this is the twentieth century, this is America, these are contemporary American poets; one would expect any small group of five of them, chosen by a single, subjective reader on the basis of both intellectual and aesthetic liking, to have at least something in common. Such is the case here. I have tried to indicate my sense of that vague commonality in the first word of my title, *uncertainty.*

I suggested earlier that we live in an age of plenitude; now I would like to put forward the (far-from-original) suggestion that we live also in an age of uncertainty, a postdeterministic age, a subjective age, an age in which we may be said to participate in the making of all aspects of our unpredictable world. The uncertainty arises from the possibility that no one is in control, that orderliness is merely an appearance, that disorderliness rules the universe, just beneath the surface of things. The possibility that we human beings may be the primary source of order in our world is quite frightening, given our propensity to mess things up. To see the mess we only have to look at the social systems generally thought to be human creations: political, economic, and other. It has been a long time since any serious person believed that we were designing these systems according to the dictates of some grand, overarching, perfectly conceived divine plan. It is the profoundly uncertain, imperfect, and unpredictable nature of these systems that has made them so often seem so idiotic, so unfair, so dangerous, so frightening.

All of that is familiar enough; the feelings of uncertainty occasioned by such systems as these will figure prominently in my essays, but all of this is old news, and none of it explains why we who live in the twentieth century are so particularly immersed in uncertainty. The reason for that has arisen only within the last eighty years: although it has always been true that our *world* is uncertain, we have only learned recently that the very basis of *reality* may also be uncertain. Before I explain what I mean more fully, I would like to define the two potentially problematic words that I have just used and that I will be using throughout this book.

When I speak of *reality*, I mean something like *that which is physically real, corporeal*—I am referring, that is, to what "actually exists" (quoting from my desk dictionary), to that which is "of a material nature; physical; perceptible by the senses; tangible"; all that is solidly, demonstrably, phenomenological. I use this word in an objective sense. My other problematical word is *world*. When I speak of "the world of John Ashbery" or "the world of Charles Wright," I mean to include everything that makes up that poet's worldview, including both such subjective elements as his understanding of politics, of religion, of economic systems, and of the objective thing I am calling reality. The reality of Ashbery's world is the same as the reality of Wright's world; everything else in their respective worlds can be different (or, possibly, the same).

Ultimately, when I use the word reality, I will be thinking of the solid stuff that is studied by physicists: physical matter, supposedly the most reliable, unchanging, least disorderly stuff of all. The basis for my assertion of uncertainty in the twentieth century is that modern physics has discovered that *stuff* is not like this after all: at its fundamental level, that is, matter is not predictable, not entirely orderly, not exactly a solid thing. Further, the way we look at this fundamental level of reality seems to play a role in determining what it *is*, meaning that what I call reality may be somewhat subjective rather than — as it used to be — entirely objective.

The idea that reality is objective was bestowed upon the world by classical physics, which itself is largely the creation of Isaac Newton. Through his formulation of the laws of gravity and motion and his development of calculus, Newton presented humankind with an orderly universe. The role of calculus is crucial to classical physics. Other mathematical systems — arithmetic, algebra, geometry, trigonometry — allow us to understand systems that are not in motion; calculus allows us to know the status of objects that are moving; it allows us, that is, to understand the effect that energy has upon objects. Once we know the status of a macrophysical system at a given moment — the position of an object (say, a planet), its mass, and its velocity — then we can know both the past status and the future status of that system. The philosophical implication inherent in classical physics is determinism, and it is determinism that flew out the window when Werner Heisenberg formulated the principle of uncertainty in 1927. We have been living with a new set of implications ever since.

Heisenberg was responding to a problem faced by physicists as they investigated the nature of the atom, which Niels Bohr had by then described as looking something like a miniature solar system. Bohr visualized the positively charged nucleus of the atom as occupying the position of the sun; surrounding it are the negatively charged electrons, which were thought to follow planetlike orbits. The next step for physics was to define more precisely the nature of these subatomic particles, and to do that physicists had to measure them; specifically, they wished to measure the location (the position) and the velocity (the energy) of these objects.

This was a classical desire, meaning that the physicists were expecting to define microphysical nature according to the inviolable laws of classical physics. All that was needed were some measurements, some exact numbers, that could be plugged into the equations. A full understanding of the system would follow. But when modern physicists attempted to measure both the position and the velocity of the electrons in an atom, they found themselves unable to establish these values at the same moment. They discovered that the more accurately they were able to measure one of these values, the less accurately they could establish the other. Some physicists questioned the instruments; perhaps in order to measure things this small it was necessary first to develop better instrumentation. But even the best instruments developed since then have made no difference, and it became obvious that the early theorists were correct: the reason for this problem is inherent within the objects being measured.

Because micronature is so different from macronature, the laws of classical physics do not apply at this micro, or quantum, level of reality: the notion that physical reality is knowable, orderly, and predictable turns out not to be true at reality's most fundamental level, the building-block level, the level of the basic stuff out of which all the rest of reality is composed. Here is why. In classical physics, matter and energy are recognized as fundamentally distinct entities: matter can possess energy, but it cannot *be* energy, except potentially; energy can act upon matter, can emerge from matter, but it cannot *be* matter. Thus, when we are measuring the status of a system at a given moment, we are establishing both the status of its matter—the position and mass of the object, for example—and its energy—the velocity of the object, for example. The basic stuff of quantum physics, however, the subatomic particles, turns out to be not a bunch of objects possessing energy but an inseparable conglomeration of energy and matter.[3] As such, they are only partially knowable at any given moment, and their future status cannot be predicted with certainty.

Classical physics came crashing down; determinism came crashing down; orderliness, predictability, certainty, physical and philosophical solidity—all these came crashing down as well. In his book *The Cosmic Code: Quantum Physics as the Language of Nature* Heinz Pagels gives a physicist's account of the philosophical implications inherent within this new understanding of reality:

> Determinism—the world view that nature and our own life are completely determined from past to future—reflects the human need for certainty in an uncertain world. The projection of that need is the all-knowing

God some people find in the Bible, a God who knows the past and future down to the finest detail—like a film that has already been developed. We may not have seen the film, but what it holds for us is already fixed.

Classical physics supported the world view of determinism. According to classical physics the laws of nature completely specify the past and future down to the finest detail. The universe was like a perfect clock: once we knew the position of its parts at one instant, they would be forever specified. . . .

With Max Born's statistical interpretation of the de Broglie–Schrödinger wave function [essentially the basis of Heisenberg's principle of uncertainty], physicists finally renounced the deterministic world view of nature. The world changed from having the determinism of a clock to having the contingency of a pinball machine. Physicists realized that the concept of the perfect all-knowing mind of God has no support in nature. Quantum theory—the new theory that replaced classical physics—makes only statistical predictions. But is there a possibility that beyond quantum theory there exists a new deterministic physics, described by some kind of subquantum theory, and the all-knowing mind uses this to determine the world? According to the quantum theory this is not possible. Even an all-knowing mind must support its knowledge with experience, and once it tries to experimentally determine one physical quantity the rest of the deck of nature gets randomly shuffled again. The very act of attempting to establish determinism produces indeterminism.[4]

Pagels is not the first thinker to assume a close relationship between physics and philosophy; in Newton's day, in fact, physicists were called natural philosophers. My argument for the importance of uncertainty to the way we think today is based on the same assumption: whether we know it or not, we (and our poets) have absorbed this attitude from the knowledge of reality presented to us by modern physics.

However, Heisenberg's formulation of the principle of uncertainty is only half the story of the philosophical importance of quantum physics. The other half involves (once again) both Bohr and Heisenberg, for the two were working together at the time, and getting in one another's hair. By February 1927, Bohr and Heisenberg had been together in Copenhagen for almost two years, trying to understand the new developments in physics. They faced two problems, and each was deeply intertwined. First was the impossibility, for a quantum situation, of giving a classical description involving two measurements: that meant that a particle was not merely a) a discrete object whose precise location could be measured, possessing b) a discrete amount of energy that could also be measured. The second problem was that the particle seemed to be composed of whichever of these two properties (matter or energy) the scientist chose to measure: if the experiment were set up to measure the position of the electron, then the position could be measured, but the velocity could not be, meaning that it did not exist and that the electron was a particle made of matter; if the experiment were set up to measure velocity, then the velocity could be measured, but the position could not be, meaning that it did not exist and that the electron was an energy wave.

Heisenberg and Bohr (and their colleagues) went round and round discussing these problems, and they got on one another's nerves. So Bohr went off on a working holiday, to think about the second problem, and Heisenberg stayed in Copenhagen, thinking about the first problem. By the time Bohr returned, he had decided that the experimenters were participating in determining the nature of the thing being measured; what they looked for they would find: reality might well be a subjective rather than an objective entity. Heisenberg, meanwhile, concluded that we will never know the exact nature of subatomic particles.

Pagels summarizes: "Heisenberg had discovered the uncertainty principle, and Bohr had discovered the principle of complementarity. Together these two principles constituted what became known as the 'Copenhagen interpretation' of quantum mechanics — an interpretation that . . . magnificently revealed the internal consistency of the quantum theory, a consistency which was purchased at the price of renouncing the determinism and objectivity of the natural world." Expanding on Bohr's contribution to the mix, Pagels goes on to emphasize that "quantum reality is in part an observer-created reality. As the physicist John Wheeler says, 'No phenomenon is a phenomenon until it is an *observed* phenomenon.'" Classical physics taught that the physical world has an objective existence outside of the observer; its laws are immutable. Under "quantum theory, [however,] human intention influences the structure of the physical world."[5]

There is another and even more profound sense in which human intention — human consciousness, perception, understanding, and expression — determines the nature of reality. What exists depends upon what we know; if we do not know something, it can hardly exist for us. What we understand depends upon what we know and how we choose to express it; if we cannot express our knowledge, then we do not understand it. Thus the way we handle "language" is crucial both to what we know and what we understand. The language of physics is mathematics; the concept of knowing in physics means being able to measure something, being able to attach a number to it. In a sense, these numbers are the words out of which understanding is woven: just as a poet combines words into lines and stanzas, with the goal of creating a full expression of his or her knowledge and understanding, so the physicist combines numbers into equations, and equations into theories, with the goal of creating a full expression of his or her knowledge and understanding. Finally, what the physicist knows and is able to explain using this complicated language is what *is*; unless the material can be expressed in this way, it cannot be said to exist for us, the human formulators.

Bohr knew this back in 1927, as Pagels reminds us: "Bohr focused on the problem of language in his interpretation of quantum mechanics. As he remarked, 'It is wrong to think that the task of physics is to find out how Nature *is*. Physics concerns what we can say about nature.'"[6] Perhaps the final word here should be given to physicist Percy Bridgman, who brilliantly summarizes the problems in knowing, understanding, and expressing that follow from the truth of the Copenhagen interpretation:

On careful examination the physicist finds that in the sense in which he uses language no meaning at all can be attached to a physical concept which cannot ultimately be described in terms of some sort of measurement. A body has position only in so far as its position can be measured; if its position cannot in principle be measured, the concept of position applied to the body is meaningless, or in other words, a position of the body does not exist. Hence if both the position and velocity of the electron cannot in principle be measured, the electron cannot have both position and velocity; position and velocity as expressions of properties which an electron can simultaneously have are meaningless. To carry the paradox one step farther, by choosing whether I shall measure the position or velocity of the electron I thereby determine whether the electron has position or velocity. The physical properties of the electron are not absolutely inherent in it, but involve also the choice of the observer.[7]

Of the poets discussed in this book, only two — John Ashbery and Charles Simic — seem to have any conscious understanding of the matters that I have been discussing, and even that is doubtful. Though I suspect Ashbery is very aware of the Copenhagen interpretation, he may not be. In any case, he does seem to approach uncertainty from the direction of reality. Simic approaches uncertainty from the direction of the world, and he knows enough about it to have said this about poets like himself and John Ashbery: "Their poetics have to do with the nature of perception, with being, with psyche, with time and consciousness. Not to subject oneself to their dialectics and uncertainties is truly not to experience the age we have inherited."[8]

The other poets I write about live in this world of uncertainty, respond to it, but they do not address it exactly as a subject; they embody uncertainty in their work and in their understanding of the world, but do not talk about doing so. They know they are creating their own subjective worlds but — except for Stephen Dobyns — they do not consciously acknowledge this fact. Dobyns seems to have built the best poems from the middle part of his career explicitly on this understanding. My approach in these essays will be somewhat similar: while I do wish to present the idea of uncertainty as a fundamental component of the worlds created by these poets — indeed, as *the* fundamental component — I do not wish to present it as the thesis of my book, something I would feel obliged to prove at every step of the way. Rather than using it as a straitjacket in which to imprison the poets, then, I will use it as the background against which to paint my portrayals of their work.

I hope that the tone of my essays will echo, however faintly, the tone of the work of these poets, for whom enjoyment seems always part of the equation. None of them is exactly a humorist, though four of them are funny at least some of the time. In fact, the amount of humor we will find in their poems seems to occur in direct proportion to the darkness of their thinking. It seems to me that Stephen Dobyns writes both the darkest and the funniest poems of these five writers. Charles Wright, who writes about sanctity and salvation, about the presence of the spiritual within the physical, writes the fewest funny passages and poems. Gerald Stern is sometimes very funny, but mostly he is buoyant: despite his feelings about the Holocaust, despite the rampant suffering he sees around him he also finds life and the worlds we live in, the natural world and the city, brimming over with the possibilities of joy. Charles Simic writes from an eastern European sensibility, mingling seriousness, cynicism, and humor: truly horrible things happen in his poems, but still he seeks, and occasionally finds, an unbearable lightness of being. John Ashbery is always a special case, whatever the point of comparison: humor is deeply but not readily present in his poems; its strength increases for the reader with each encounter, and it is most apparent when one hears Ashbery reading his own poems.

What these poets share as a group, then, is my admiration and their residence in America during the age of uncertainty, the age of muchness. Yes, the age of muchness is also the age of uncertainty, and how could it be otherwise? Perhaps the reason this is an age of muchness is that it is the age of uncertainty. With no intellectual, conceptual, philosophical steadiness to guide us, we cannot choose from among the elements of plenitude. Everything becomes equal, and everything proliferates; nothing is ruled out, so nothing is able to rule; nothingness comes to live at our core. Ultimately, then, these poets share little of substance beyond what I define as their quality. Lacking a positive centrality, a positive pole, they seem unable to gather their worlds with certainty around them; they have no sure sense of controlling their worlds, no sense that they can make sense of it all. And that is why they will remain different from one another, even after I am done discussing them; that is why this book has no dominating, cohesive, singular thesis. So let me tell you something more about my take on each of these poets — my *alphabetical* take on these poets, for that is how I have ordered them.

Perhaps the most important poet of our age, John Ashbery writes about everything and nothing. Of the poets discussed in this book, he is the one most aware of his lack of understanding. The speaker of his poems approaches the world ever in wonder, finding all of it fascinating, charming, enticing; but he has little or no idea of what it means. He is attracted to objects, to places, to situations; he describes things in loving detail, he tells stories, he creates interesting locales. We do not know what he prefers, for he prefers all and none; he is uncertain, he cannot make up his mind, he will take them all. He is similarly attracted to ideas, ideas from everywhere, on any and every subject, and again he seems not to choose, again he uses them all. He writes a poetry of acceptance and mingling; he creates a world of conflicting and harmonious multitudes, a universe of poetic muchness and plenitude.

Thus he drives a certain type of reader to distraction. The certain type I mean is still common in our age, particularly perhaps among our critics: a reader in search of certainties, a reader who wants poets to have a cohesive, coherent vision of things. Perhaps not knowing what it all means, such a reader wants to be told what it means. None of the poets I am discussing is truly able to do that, and Ashbery is least able of all. But his grandfather was a professor of physics at the University of Rochester, and Ashbery lived in this man's home for significant portions of his youth. Perhaps that is why he seems to gravitate instinctively to Heisenberg's principle of uncertainty. So suffused by this principle is Ashbery's thinking that he will not admit even to knowing about it (a cunningly uncertain gesture), much less knowing where he learned it. Ashbery is posing all the time: in this case, methinks he doth protest too much.

The poems of Stephen Dobyns are clearer than those of Ashbery, easier to interpret and understand. But what I primarily see when I look at his work is a confused, uncertain, and searching man, given to depression. I am describing not Stephen Dobyns directly but the speaker, the narrator, of his poems. Given this character's uncertainty, it may seem odd that Dobyns should be the most didactic of these poets, the one most given to establishing theses in his poems, the one most enamored of teaching us lessons. And what a bunch of lessons they are! The speaker in Dobyns' poems is obsessed by the futility of human life, by its meaninglessness; obsessed by our inability to know what is going on, our inability to control it; obsessed by our frail and imperfect bodies, by the certainty that they will die and turn to dust. He is often crippled by nostalgia, by the carefree times of the past, the questionless times, the times when life was calm and he was in love and was loved in return. All of which may make Dobyns sound like an unreadable poet, an arrogant emperor of dreariness and self-pity. But his poems are rarely dreary, almost never uninteresting, often funny, and nearly always fun; they are narrative based, and Dobyns, who is also a successful novelist, tells resonant, poignant, pointed, and amusing stories.

Charles Simic is probably the most cosmopolitan of the poets discussed in this book; certainly he is the most political, the one most familiar with that particularly dangerous realm of uncertainty. Because he grew up in Yugoslavia during the Second World War, Simic has a close personal knowledge of the dark realities of twentieth-century politics. He expresses this awareness in poems that are clipped, oblique, allusive, minimalist — but also witty, even surprisingly funny, given his usual range of subject matter. Simic's favorite literary device, the metaphor, is also the one that affords him his greatest ambition: because it can be used to link objects and thoughts that are not just slightly different but even fundamentally different from one another, Simic believes that metaphor can be his means of reaching to the mysterious essence of being. It is upon this metaphysical ambition that critic Helen Vendler bases her condemnation of Simic's work, to which I shall reply in my essay.

Though Gerald Stern also writes, sometimes, about such twentieth-century atrocities as the Holocaust, the tone, voice, and rhythms of his poetry are very different from those of Simic. Stern is our Walt Whitman, the Walt Whitman of our age, though perhaps I should identify him only as my contemporary Walt Whitman, since so many poets — Allen Ginsberg, C. K. Williams, Philip Schultz, Galway Kinnell, and others — have been identified as our contempo-

rary Whitman. Stern sings expansively of himself within a large and complicated world, a world with a long, troubling, and wonderful history, a world of
cities and of nature, of street people and of trees, birds, hermits, fish platters,
root beer, and soap. His poems are open and inclusive, as huge and buoyant as
those of Simic are brief, indirect, and sly.

If this book discusses a poet who is an exception to its general rule, then that
poet is Charles Wright. What makes him unique is the balance of his focus,
which leans toward the positive notion of the presence of essence, of being,
of something spiritual at the heart of nature, rather than toward the power of
uncertainty. My angle of entry to his work is through the idea of a baroque
style — something he shares with Stanley Kunitz — and through Wright's own
notion of deep form. The differences between Kunitz and Wright are probably
deeper than their similarities. Kunitz is thirty years older than Wright, is from
a large northern city rather than a small southern city, and is firmly grounded
in the everyday and in the historical and mythological past rather than in the
aesthetic present used as a springboard into the unseen. What they have in
common is a love of intricate patterns of language and of exotic figuration, a
propensity for extravagant metaphor, a habit of comparing such things as sun-
sets and oranges, fishes and nails, Worcester, Massachusetts, and the city of the
burning cloud, Torri del Benaco, on the shore of Lake Garda, and Kingsport,
Tennessee.

At that deeper level, Wright may share more with Charles Simic than with
Stanley Kunitz. Like Simic, but more strongly, Wright believes that poetry can
reach toward essence, toward truth, toward a modicum of harmony and certainty. He began his career interested almost purely in style — in words considered as words, as manipulable things in themselves — but gradually has moved
to a far deeper, more comprehensive and meaningful notion of form. In his
mature work he sees language not as a discrete world of reality, or as creative of
a discrete world of reality, but as inherently metaphorical, as inseparably tied to
the world. He handles objects in a similar fashion: the images in his poems
rarely remain singularly referential to the things they describe but almost always take on the power of metaphor, relating object to object, or object to notion. Thus might words and objects together open a window into the meta-

physical essence of the physical world. But only might; the fact that he is never certain that this method actually works is what ultimately ties Wright to the rest of the poets in this book. In the final analysis, he is not truly an exception to my rule; he too resides in a world of uncertainty.

It remains for me to thank the many people from whom I have received encouragement, advice, insight, and practical assistance during the time that I was writing this book. The list of my colleagues at Gettysburg College to whom I am indebted is too long to be given completely, but I will mention two groups that have been especially helpful. First, I would like to thank Jeff Mock, Emily Ruark Clarke, Linda Stonesifer, Cathy Staneck, and Carolyn R. Guss, my colleagues at the *Gettysburg Review*, whose dedication and hard work have allowed me the ease of mind necessary to write this book. Second, I would like to thank Robert S. Fredrickson, chair of the Department of English; Baird Tipson, former provost of the college; Gordon Haaland, president of the college; Janet Riggs, former acting-provost of the college; and Dan DeNicola, current provost of the college, all of whom helped make it possible for me to accept a fellowship from the National Endowment for the Humanities. Without the assistance of the NEH, this manuscript almost certainly would never have been finished; I thank them for the financial assistance that allowed me the time free of my teaching duties during which I was able to complete my work.

Several persons have read and commented on portions of this manuscript in various of its versions. In particular I would like to thank Stanley Lindberg, editor of the *Georgia Review*, who helped me clarify my earliest readings of some of these poets; Bob Fredrickson (again), who, in addition to making my life easier in his role as chair of my department, also read earlier drafts of some of these essays and helped me make them better; Donald Hall, who did his best over the years to encourage me at the same time as he tried to rein me in, pull me back from adventures beyond my ken; Floyd Collins, who read and commented helpfully upon some of these essays, and whose own readings of some of the poets helped me to clarify mine; Paul Zimmer, who has been an ever-patient counselor, editor, and friend; Laurence A. Marschall, professor of physics at Gettysburg College, who vetted the more technical parts of this introduction; and John Winship, who read my manuscript in several versions, helping make each one a little better. While these readers may be responsible for some of the strengths of my work, I hope that none of them will be held accountable for any weaknesses it may possess.

Throughout the years that I have been working on this book, I have benefited as well from the insights of students in my seminars on contemporary poetry, offered at Middlebury College many years ago, at the University of Houston, and more recently at Gettysburg College. In particular, I would like to mention Eve Ensler, Susan Hong, Warren Koons, Paul McDonough, Catherine Pfaff, and Patrick Regan; Michelle Boisseau, Nancy Chamberlain, Nancy Eimers, Jeffrey Greene, Stella Johnston, Richard Lyons, Martin McGovern, Mark Miller, Gary Myers, William Olsen, Arthur Smith, Gail Donohue Storey, James Ulmer, and Sidney Wade; Sandra Agostinho, Brian Black, Kelly Celesky, Helen Devinney, Amy DiGiovanni, Robert Doggett, Christina Folz, Erin Francy, Matthew Getty, Paul Haaland, Holly Lavieri, Robin Pascucci, Jennifer Remeikis, and Ken Rodriguez.

I would also like to thank the other critics who have written on these poets and from whose publications I have benefited. Most of them are recognized more specifically in the notes to this volume, which will supply curious readers with a bibliography of other sources to consult on these poets. I have also used the notes, when appropriate, to argue with some of these critics, to extend some of my discussions, even to argue occasionally with myself.

John
Ashbery

The Poetics of Uncertainty

John Ashbery brings out the best and the worst in people who care about contemporary American poetry. The best is exemplified by the reception he has gotten throughout the years from the officialdom of poetry: so many awards, so much honor, such a plenitude of vociferous praise, so many plaques, so many laurel wreaths, so many barrels of cash. His first book, *Some Trees*, was selected by W. H. Auden for publication in the Yale Series of Younger Poets in 1956. More recently, as the dust jacket to his *Selected Poems* tells us, "His 1975 volume, *Self-Portrait in a Convex Mirror*, won the Pulitzer Prize, the National Book Award, and the National Book Critics Circle Award. He is a member of the National Academy and Institute of Arts and Letters and the National Academy of Arts and Sciences. Twice named a Guggenheim Fellow, he was awarded the annual fellowship of the Academy of American Poets in 1982. In 1985 he received a MacArthur Prize Fellowship." Currently he is a chancellor of the Academy of American Poets.

What makes this muchness of recognition odd is the fact that so many serious readers of poetry seem to have no idea of what Ashbery's poems are about. Robert Boyers, for example, has spoken of the frustration he feels when trying to teach Ashbery's poems to undergraduate students:

Some of us have tried, with small success, to explain Ashbery in the class-room, concluding that a great many complete poems, and large portions of others, resist any kind of explanation. Other more gifted interpreters have concluded that even where ordinary readings work, they discover nothing of genuine consequence in Ashbery's thought.[1]

Boyers' last comment (which has the distinction of being both a left-handed compliment and a cliché of much of the criticism devoted to Ashbery's work) has a certain accuracy, if one is willing to accept the rather odd notion that some ideas in works of art are more important than others. Thus we might say that some of Ashbery's poems do indeed seem as inconsequential as they are comprehensible, for example, "The Instruction Manual," which I will discuss later. But it seems equally true that other of his poems are both comprehensible and intellectually challenging, as Laurence Lieberman has demonstrated in his excellent discussion of the poem "Self-Portrait in a Convex Mirror."[2] This is a minor point, however, compared to the error Boyers makes when he assumes that Ashbery — apparently as all good poets ought to do — wishes to make tra-ditional thematic sense in most or all of his poems. Such is simply not the case.

What, if anything, Ashbery does wish to say — or, more accurately, what he wishes to accomplish — in his work is a complex matter that needs to be ad-dressed from several perspectives. We might begin by considering the way meaning is achieved or perhaps avoided in "Two Scenes," the first of Ashbery's poems that most readers are likely to encounter: it appears both on the open-ing page of *Some Trees* and on the opening page of his *Selected Poems*, pub-lished almost thirty years later in 1985. The poem is appropriate to my exercise for two other reasons: it is relatively short, which means we will have an easy time keeping its details in mind, and it is typical of Ashbery's practice generally. Each of the scenes is presented in a single stanza, and I will comment on them in order:

We see us as we truly behave:
From every corner comes a distinctive offering.

The train comes bearing joy;
The sparks it strikes illuminate the table.
Destiny guides the water-pilot, and it is destiny.
For long we hadn't heard so much news, such noise.
The day was warm and pleasant.
"We see you in your hair,
Air resting around the tips of mountains."

The first two lines seem to invite the reader into a poem about the revealing behavior of an "us," perhaps the poet and a friend or friends, perhaps the poet
and his readers. The first piece of specific evidence to appear, however, is not a
"distinctive offering" of a way "we truly behave," but a train that bears joy and
strikes table-illuminating sparks.

The logic is puzzling, and it seems clear that, if readers want these first two
sentences to cohere, then they are going to have to supply something from
their own imagination. So let's say that, perhaps, Ashbery is writing about a
childhood Christmas morning: presents everywhere and, best of all, an electric
train! Unfortunately, the next line does not support this reading; it also does
not build upon the image of the train, being about a water-pilot rather than
about a railroad engineer. Again our hunger for coherence is unfulfilled. Then
we learn that a lot of noise and information are coming in — on a nice day. The
final two lines seem to create a bizarre image of someone's head being like the
tip of a mountain surrounded by air that resembles hair, but we know neither
who says this nor why. The stanza seems built on the appearance of logic, of
cause and effect, but with no internal substance to support it. No wonder a
reader might feel misled.

In the second scene, Ashbery seems to organize his details into a narrative
structure spanning time from day into evening. Once again, however, a close
look reveals more discontinuity than continuity:

A fine rain anoints the canal machinery.
This is perhaps a day of general honesty

Without example in the world's history
Though the fumes are not of a singular authority
And indeed are dry as poverty.
Terrific units are on an old man
In the blue shadow of some paint cans
As laughing cadets say, "In the evening
Everything has a schedule, if you can find out what it is."

The first line is promising: in the opening scene we had a water-pilot guided by destiny; does the pilot perhaps ply his trade on the canal whose machinery is here being anointed by a fine rain? That would be nice, but alas, nothing else in the poem either supports or denies this possibility. Similarly, in the first scene, the day is warm and pleasant; here we have, first, a fine rain, then a singular degree of honesty — inexplicably undercut by some fumes — then an old man shadowed by paint cans. Do those shadows mean the day has suddenly turned sunny? Why are the shadows blue? And why is it *cadets* who are so certain there must be a schedule: why not midshipmen, or first-year students, or painters deemed to be members of the New York School? The most striking word in the stanza, indeed in the poem, is *units*, but what does it refer to?

Ashbery gives the reader no way to know the answers to these questions, no sure way to connect the details. Indeed, he seems almost intent upon making us bark up the wrong trees (perhaps these are the "some trees" of the book title). Rather than base his poem on logic, he seems to be basing it on illogic, wanting to tantalize and fool us, wanting to pull something funny. According to David Shapiro, this is exactly what happens in many of the poems: Ashbery is using a technique learned from the French novelist and poet Raymond Roussel (1877–1933), on whose work he once began writing a doctoral thesis: "In lieu of the organic and necessary simile, Ashbery learned from the French master an extravagance of connection that leads one nowhere. . . . Ashbery is also a master of the false summation, the illogical conclusion couched in the jargon of logic and reminiscent of the false but rich scholarship of Borges."[3] "Two Scenes" seems clearly based on this constructional notion — a seemingly random, ultimately meaningless, inherently amusing juxtaposition of unrelated details.

If the progress of the poem is not determined by meaning, then perhaps it is determined by some notion of form. Ashbery does show a great deal of interest in matters of pure form, particularly in his early work. For example, a surprising number of the poems in *Some Trees*—"Pantoum," "Canzone," "Poem," "The Painter," "A Pastoral," and others—are written in verbally redundant French forms, almost as though Ashbery were trying them on for size. As I hope I will be able to demonstrate in a moment through an analysis of "The Painter," most of these poems gradually lose in coherence of meaning what they maintain in rigor of form. It is tempting to conclude, then, that Ashbery wishes to achieve in "Two Scenes" as in many of his other poems something like what Flaubert, in a letter to Louise Colet, said he would like to achieve in a novel:

> What seems beautiful to me, what I should like to write, is a book about nothing, a book dependent on nothing external, which would be held together by the strength of its style, just as the earth, suspended in the void, depends on nothing external for its support; a book which would have almost no subject, or at least in which the subject is almost invisible, if such a thing is possible.[4]

This seems almost right as a description of some of Ashbery's work, but not quite. It is too abstract, for one thing, too idealized, too romantic, too unearthly; it lacks the tantalizing effect we see in the poems, and it seems to offer no promise of humor. A more accurate description is one given—not surprisingly—by Ashbery himself. In 1957, only a year after the publication of his first book, he said this about a volume by Gertrude Stein:

> *Stanzas in Meditation* gives one the feeling of time passing, of things happening, of a "plot," though it would be difficult to say precisely what is going on. Sometimes the story has the logic of a dream ... while at other times it becomes startlingly clear for a moment, as though a change in the wind

had suddenly enabled us to hear a conversation that was taking place some distance away. . . . But it is usually not events which interest Miss Stein, rather it is their "way of happening."[5]

Precisely. One often has the impression of a controlling plot or thesis at the beginning of an Ashbery poem, but this feeling is likely to break down rather quickly as we become aware that the poet's focus is not on the overall pattern of the poem, the pattern of its details, but on those details themselves, their "way of happening." As Dana Gioia has said of Ashbery at midcareer: "One never remembers ideas from an Ashbery poem, one recalls the tones and textures. If ideas are dealt with at all, they are present only as faint echoes heard remotely in some turn of phrase. Ideas in Ashbery are like the melodies in some jazz improvisation where the musicians have left out the original tune to avoid paying royalties."[6]

If meaning truly exists for Ashbery (and there is some doubt), then it seems to have a local relevance only, a temporary and uncertain relevance; most certainly it seems not to have a grand or encompassing relevance, a metaphysical relevance. We will find Ashbery to be extremely suspicious, even contemptuous, of claims to general truth, as is apparent in a biting comment he once made on the poetry of Philip Booth: "Rare is the grain of sand in which he can't spot the world; seagulls, dories, and schools of herring are likewise windows on eternity, until we begin to suspect that he is in direct, hot-line communication with it."[7] Ashbery does not use objects or images in his poems as symbolic windows onto the landscape of eternity, and for a simple enough reason: he seems quite clearly to believe that eternity does not *have* a landscape. David Fite has recognized how radically different Ashbery's method is from that of Booth: "Ashbery's personifications . . . very seldom address natural objects precisely because the natural object does not, for him, furnish a symbolical road to the sublime."[8]

The world in which Ashbery lives is extremely different from the world inhabited by Philip Booth, which happens to be the world inhabited by most other contemporary poets, a meaningful world, a world based on a scheme — or on a schedule, a schedule that the poet-cadet may be able to uncover if he or she looks hard enough, composes harmoniously enough. It is, in short, the world of classical physics, a world in which determinism is in charge, a world of order, of cause and effect, of certain (though perhaps hidden) significance. Is it any wonder, then, that the typical contemporary poet writes poems that are likely both to be coherent in their form and to pursue a fundamental level of meaning that may well be coherent also?

Ashbery's poems are not generally like this; the world that he sees around him makes so little sense that it seems never to occur to him to look for a deeper level of meaning. Indeed, he is contemptuous of undertaking such a search. Ashbery's poems emerge from a different world, a world in which poetry—in the words of David Shapiro—"has indeed become, as Robert Delaunay said of art, something shattered as the fruit-dish of Cézanne. And why? Because the truth itself has shattered into something relative and nomadic. Because our poetry now must be a self-portrait of poetry in the most shattering of mirrors."[9]

Rather than a pursuit of conventional significance, what we find in the poetry of Ashbery is an interest in language and in the question of form; an interest in the nature of poetry itself, especially the process through which it comes into being; an interest in incongruity and humor; an interest in the self, in individual consciousness, in particular patterns of thought and ways of thinking; an interest—since there is no such thing as a cosmic truth of meaning—in the local truth of detail, situation, and character; an interest in the power of the perceiving imagination to create the world; and an interest, therefore, in the likelihood that the world in which we live is, as Heisenberg and Bohr said in their Copenhagen interpretation, uncertain, indeterminate, and subjective.

Ashbery is perhaps the purest example of a Copenhagenist thinker in all of American literature; his poems seem almost designed with Heisenberg's principle of uncertainty in mind. With little deviation, he has embodied this vision in nearly all of his work. Which leads to a lovely irony: because Ashbery's vision is so deeply suspicious of our ability to know the truth about the world in a traditional sense, the question of meaning, of making sense, becomes an unusually important issue facing the reader or critic of Ashbery. I will therefore be spending much of my time in this essay talking about meaning in Ashbery's poems, and often this will mean talking about the absence of meaning in them, or the radically oblique meanings in them. It seems ironic that one should spend so much time interpreting the poems of a poet who seems not to believe in meaning—except that Ashbery's refusal to believe in meaning is itself meaningful.

Inevitably, my interpretations, like the poems themselves, will be speculative, imaginative, and uncertain. How could they possibly be otherwise? As David Shapiro has said, "'Understanding,' which most readers of poetry have been trained by generations of text-analysers to believe is the object of reading, can be extracted from an Ashbery poem only at the price of distortion."[10] The interpretations that I will offer may well be distortions; indeed, I take it as axiomatic that they probably will not be "correct." But I also take it as axiomatic that no interpretation of an Ashbery poem is ultimately correct; indeed, it may well be that no single interpretation of any poem is ultimately correct.

Thus the process of interpretation that I intend to follow is arguably as valid as any other process. Ashbery himself seemed to demonstrate the truth of this point during an interview that I did with him on behalf of the *Paris Review*. In response to my question about the problem of meaning in his poems, Ashbery replied: "Many critics tend to want to see an allegorical meaning in every concrete statement, and if we just choose a line at random, I think we will find this isn't the way it works. . . . I can't seem to find anything that's an example of what I mean. Well, let's take this . . . no. Everything I look at does seem to mean something other than what is being said, all of a sudden."[11] Setting out to prove that his poems have no meaning beyond what they say, Ashbery found that every poem that he looked at had meaning beyond what it said. And then, of course, he found the example he was looking for. The incident illustrates nicely the inescapable hegemony of uncertainty, over poet and critic alike.

Another poem from Ashbery's first book illustrates this in a particularly profound way. "The Painter" seems to enact, indirectly to be sure, both the drama and the significance inherent in our passage from a view of the world based on classical physics to a view of the world based on quantum physics. Before I look at "The Painter," however, I want to say something about Wallace Stevens' "The Idea of Order at Key West." Among all the poets who have influenced Ashbery, Stevens seems the one who has influenced him the most.

Indeed, "The Painter" seems even to have been written with "The Idea of Order at Key West" in mind. Rather than interpret Stevens' poem — which I am sure is familiar to most of my readers — I am going to present and comment on the "Notes toward an interpretation" given by John Frederick Nims in his wonderful book *The Harper Anthology of Poetry*. Nims' comment points toward the standard (and most probably correct) interpretation of the poem, in which

> two voices are heard, that of the sea, and that of a girl singing beside it. The first is inhuman, mindless, meaningless. The second is human, mindful, meaningful; its words interpret what the sea might be imagined as saying. It gives form to the formless, order to the disorderly. The human mind, that is, through its art, gives order and significance to a universe that has neither. Just as, when we look at the stars, we see patterns, constellations, so when we look at the lights of fishing boats in the harbor we see geometric patterns they impose on the night. Our human "rage for order" demands that we organize the chaos of experience. Stevens said that in the poem "life has ceased to be a matter of chance. It may be that every man introduces his own order into the life about him. . . . These are tentative ideas for the purposes of poetry." [12]

The singing young woman, through her song, brings order to an apparently disordered reality, much as Isaac Newton did through his invention of calculus. The difference between the two actions is that Newton believed he was describing reality accurately — that is, it really is orderly beneath its appearance of disorder — while Stevens seems to think that reality remains disorderly, despite the song. For Stevens, poems stand apart from reality, though they are based upon it; they have the miraculous power to make order where there is no order. Reality does not have this power.

Ashbery agrees with Stevens about the inherent uncertainty of reality, but he disagrees with him about the "miraculous" power of poetry to create an orderly version of this perplexing mess. The artist in his poem is a painter, not a singer; the sea is still the sea, a disorderly, rowdy, unpredictable, but still fascinating and aesthetically enticing uncooked soup. In the first stanza, the painter adopts a naively Newtonian position:

> Sitting between the sea and the buildings
> He enjoyed painting the sea's portrait.
> But just as children imagine a prayer
> Is merely silence, he expected his subject
> To rush up the sand, and, seizing a brush,
> Plaster its own portrait on the canvas.

The picture that classical physics paints of reality is the picture that reality itself would paint, had it this power of expression. Neither a physicist nor a mathematician, our naive painter expects the sea to do all the work for him: since the sea is already orderly, it can paint its own portrait just by throwing itself onto the canvas. Unfortunately, Ashbery tells us, the painter misunderstands how these things work: he is like those "children" who "imagine a prayer / Is merely silence," while the silent adults, their heads bowed in church, are working hard to create their own versions of reality, which they wish to express to the supposed receiver of their prayers. Those prayers are like poems, or paintings, or mathematical theories: some creative activity on the part of the human mind is required to bring them into being. Unaware of this important step, the childish artist merely lounges on the beach waiting for a wave to fall.

In the second stanza, "the people who lived in the buildings" offer their advice: "Try using the brush / As a means to an end," they say; "Select . . . / Something less angry and large, and more subject / To a painter's moods, or, perhaps, to a prayer." The advice is awkwardly stated, not altogether clear; we notice that the precision of expression that Ashbery achieved in his first stanza is beginning to break down. And for an important and obvious reason: because he is writing a sestina, Ashbery is not entirely in control of his poem. He is required to write seven stanzas, the first six of which are to be six lines long while the seventh must be three lines long. The end words of the lines of the first stanza must become the end words, following a rigid pattern that determines their placement, of the lines of the next five stanzas. In the concluding stanza, these same words must be repeated as the middle and end words of the three lines. Once he has written his first stanza, we might say, Ashbery's destiny is taken over by a rigidly predetermined pattern, a Newtonian pattern, that specifies not only what words he must use, but where he must use them. I will comment later on the significance of this choice of form; for now I wish to return to the content of the poem.

At the start of the third stanza, the painter reasserts his dream — "his prayer / That nature, not art, might usurp the canvas" — but then takes the advice of the onlookers by attempting a portrait of his wife, "Making her vast, like ruined buildings, / As if, forgetting itself, the portrait / Had expressed itself without a brush." The logic is circular: still wishing that nature would express itself directly on his canvas, the painter decides instead to take control himself, with the result that "the portrait . . . express[es] itself without a brush." Since the painter has no idea of what he is or is not doing, the question arises, does the wife really look like "vast . . . ruined buildings," or is she somehow coming to resemble the sea?

However we choose to answer this question, the painter is enough encouraged by his success to attempt, in the fourth stanza, another portrait of the sea:

Slightly encouraged, he dipped his brush
In the sea, murmuring a heartfelt prayer:
"My soul, when I paint this next portrait
Let it be you who wrecks the canvas."
The news spread like wildfire through the buildings:
He had gone back to the sea for his subject.

The painter's prayer seems to show him back on the right track. His desire to involve his soul indicates a willingness to do what Stevens' singer did: create, using his imagination and his intelligence, his own version of the reality that lies before him. But even while saying this, he dips his brush not into his paints but into the water, once again hoping that the sea will paint itself!

And so, again and inevitably, he fails, as we see in the fifth stanza:

Imagine a painter crucified by his subject!
Too exhausted even to lift his brush,
He provoked some artists leaning from the buildings
To malicious mirth: "We haven't a prayer
Now, of putting ourselves on canvas,
Or getting the sea to sit for a portrait!"

These "artists," looking at the pathetic efforts of a mere "painter," are undoubtedly being ironic. In truth, they do not for a second believe that his failure lessens their ability to fulfill their prayer, that the soul should determine the painting. The irony continues into the sixth stanza, which begins with "Others [among the artists] declar[ing] it a self-portrait." Oh, bitter, that the painter's pathetic masterpiece—in which "all indications of a subject / Began to fade, leaving the canvas / Perfectly white"—should be not only his creation, but a mirror unto himself.

The painter has completely failed in his Newtonian project: to allow nature to reveal its own grand order. Not only does nature turn out not to be orderly, it turns out also not to have a mind with which to express its disorder. All of this is consonant, albeit in a negative fashion, with what Stevens says in "The Idea of Order at Key West": order can be supplied only by the creative intelligence, the imagination, of the artist. But Stevens' poem arrives at this conclusion through the poet's creation of his own appropriate form; Stevens, in other words, enacts in his own song the process that he describes using the young woman singing on the beach: both of them create order from disorder.

Ashbery, on the other hand, creates disorder from order. What is really Newtonian in this poem, what really reminds us of the world of classical physics, is not the efforts of the painter but the poet's choice of a rigid, predetermined form. The actions of reality, we recall Newton telling us, follow such forms: once we know exactly the details of a physical situation, we can predict its future status by applying inviolable laws. In his first stanza, Ashbery establishes the exact details of the situation he intends to develop. All that is required in the rest of the poem is a rigorous application to that situation of the inviolable rules that govern the writing of a sestina. The result is that the system fails utterly, as the poem's final stanza illustrates so beautifully. By now the painter's neighbors and fellow artists have had enough of him and his foolery:

> They tossed him, the portrait, from the tallest of the buildings;
> And the sea devoured the canvas and the brush
> As though his subject had decided to remain a prayer.

This stanza is almost completely arbitrary in what it says; Ashbery, perhaps the best poet of our time, is reduced to having the abilities of a sixth-grade writer. The ultimate meaning of the poem is to be found in this formal fact rather than in what the stanza says. Rather than build coherently to an inevitable and predictable conclusion, the poem instead gradually loses intensity, loses focus, loses cohesion, loses all of the sense of certainty with which it began. Whether Ashbery designed the poem to work in this way or not, this is the way in which it does work.

Not many poets write sestinas anymore, and for what I think is an obvious reason. We might say that the sestina, like other rigid and predetermined forms, is a relic of its age, the age of determinism, the age of classical (Newtonian) physics, the age in which all knowledge of the physical world was certain knowledge, predetermined knowledge. As such it has little relevance to our age of uncertainty, the age of quantum physics. Translating the situation of writing a sestina into the language of physics, it is as though the results of the experiment were known before it was begun, that all of the measurements the physicist was hoping to discover were already known. In such a situation discovery becomes virtually impossible for both physicist and poet: with word choice being so limited, so governed by rigid requirements, the poet is either going to arrive at a predetermined meaning or (more likely) at no meaning, a foolish meaning, or a meaningless meaning. Such is the case with "The Painter."

Thus Ashbery agrees with Stevens that reality lacks order, but seems to disagree with him — at least here — that the process of art can do any better at establishing order. He intentionally tests one of the most orderly of all poetic forms against the power of disorder, and disorder wins. The lesson is that poetry cannot be expected to behave much differently than reality: they are both unpredictable, uncontrollable, indeterminate, inherently uncertain. At least this is what they are some of the time; obviously there are exceptions to this pattern among Ashbery's poems. But at least here we find him to be a mimetic poet, a poet who wishes to reproduce the lessons of reality accurately in his poems.

"The Painter" is an objective poem to the degree that it presents its meaning through a character other than either its author or its speaker. Mimesis in this poem is thus an especially tricky matter, since it involves the poet's ironic commentary on his own form. Elsewhere — in his more subjective poems — we will find it an easier topic to address, as Peter Hainsworth has noticed: "Ashbery is a radically mimetic artist who aims to reproduce experience as directly as possible, while making it plain that the gap between words and things is infinite: reality has always passed on, or at least is absent from what we are reading." [13] The experience that Ashbery deals with in his poems is not what we ordinarily think of as experience. Rather than deal with the events that happen to us within the world of physical reality, Ashbery writes of these things as they are registered by the mind; he himself has said, "I'm trying to set down a generalized transcript of what's really going on in our minds all day long." [14] He is a poet of perceptions rather than of events and actual objects, and just as our attention passes quickly from impression to impression, often without any sort of completion, coherence, or connection, so do his poems.

I speak of "our attention"; Ashbery speaks of "our minds." It does appear that he wishes his poems to be somehow broadly representative of the way we all think and register impressions; one often feels that the presiding consciousness of Ashbery's poems is transparent, merely a neutral conduit of impressions. But perhaps this consciousness is specifically that of Ashbery himself. A short time after he wondered, during the interview that I did with him, "if I am suffering from some mental dysfunction because of how weird and baffling my poetry seems to so many people and sometimes to me too," I asked him about the voice that speaks his poems:

It doesn't seem to me like my voice. I have had many arguments about this with my analyst, who is actually a South American concert pianist, more interested in playing the piano than in being a therapist. He says, "Yes, I know, you always think that these poems come from somewhere else. You refuse to realize that it is really you that is writing the poems and not having them dictated by some spirit somewhere." It is hard for me to realize that because I have such an imprecise impression of what kind of person I am.[15]

Often the reader feels the presence of more than one consciousness directing the progress of an Ashbery poem; for Thomas Fink, this is one of the truest sources of Ashbery's humor: "Ashbery uses incongruities produced by an irreducibly double perspective (as opposed to a relentless single focus) to make sure that a predominantly comic textual atmosphere prevails over the possibilities of anguish or staid seriousness. This doubleness does not foster a 'New Critical' balance or 'reconciliation of opposites'; the humor 'spotlights' the incompleteness of any one viewpoint, attitude, or synthesis."[16]

At other times Ashbery achieves both humor and transparency through the use of an almost simpleminded speaker, someone who seems incapable of reflection, incapable of doing anything more than gathering impressions. Such a speaker narrates "The Instruction Manual," also from *Some Trees*, which begins:

> As I sit looking out of a window of the building
> I wish I did not have to write the instruction manual on the uses of a new
>   metal.
> I look down into the street and see people, each walking with an inner
>   peace,
> And envy them — they are so far away from me!
> Not one of them has to worry about getting out this manual on schedule.
> And, as my way is, I begin to dream, resting my elbows on the desk and
>   leaning out of the window a little,
> Of dim Guadalajara! City of rose-colored flowers!
> City I most wanted to see, and most did not see, in Mexico!

The humor comes from this character's totally unreflective ditziness, which produces at least three lovely jokes in just these lines. First is the ridiculousness of writing such a manual; only when a metal has been around for a long time does anyone know enough about it to describe its uses. Second, the description of Guadalajara as the "City of rose-colored flowers" is wonderfully, floridly absurd. Third is the speaker's undercutting of his own position, and of our confidence in him, in the last-quoted line above; has he or has he not, we wonder, actually been to Guadalajara? One could reply that of course he has been there; this is just his way of saying he did not plumb to the heart of the place. But the rest of the poem is so detailed that we cannot doubt his insight; we therefore conclude that perhaps Ashbery wants us to think his speaker is imagining all this. Most likely of all, however, is that Ashbery wants us not to be sure precisely what is true, just as the central consciousness of his poems so often seems not sure of what is really going on.[17]

Another way of saying that Ashbery's focus is on the details rather than on the plot is to say that his focus is on the words of his poems rather than on the reality to which those words may be said to refer. Indeed, David Spurr sees Ashbery's poems as self-contained linguistic structures bearing little or no relationship to the outer world: "Ashbery's poetry calls forth a notion of language as an infinite series of gestures tied to each other as a system of arbitrary signs, yet connected to no external, extra-linguistic reality. Ashbery represents language as constitutive rather than reflective of reality, implying a collapse of the ordinary hierarchical distinction between signifier and signified."[18] A closely related factor aiding Ashbery in his seeming, sometimes goal of not making sense is his love of the pure image, the unattached metaphor. Taken together, these factors lead to some of Ashbery's most nonreferential works.

Good examples occur in the series of short poems, "37 Haiku," printed in Ashbery's late book *A Wave* (1984); two of the more puzzling read: "You have original artworks hanging on the walls oh I said edit" and "A blue anchor grains of grit in a tall sky sewing." Traditional haiku form requires a total of seventeen syllables divided into three lines of five, seven, and five. The first "haiku" here has eighteen syllables, and the second has thirteen, in each case presented in a single, proselike line. All of Ashbery's so-called haiku are one prosey line long, and none of them ends with a period. Perhaps this use of form is itself a kind of nonreferential metaphor. Of the two that I have quoted, the first is easier to interpret—but only in an interpolative way: perhaps it means that the walls have too many artworks, and some should be taken down. Since Ashbery was a painter during his adolescence and has been an art critic for much of his adult life, the sentiment is probably not his; thus interpretation becomes more complex, as we must introduce either irony or a separate speaker or both into the discussion. But clearly the poem is not worth these pains; it is an isolated fragment bearing no discernable relationship, beyond a loose resemblance of form, to the fragments around it. We might best conclude, then, that the poem is a word- or image-construct rather than a meaning-construct. Such an approach is even more obviously appropriate to the second haiku, which truly seems to establish or inhabit a world of its own devising.

Perhaps most obviously, neither of these little poems may be said to plunge us to a deeper level of reality; neither of them is, in short, "surreal." It has been the habit of shallow readers of poetry in the twentieth century, confronted by poems they cannot understand, to call them surreal; in reviews in the popular press—and sometimes in the not-so-popular press—Ashbery has often been called a surrealist. However, the true surrealists, in France, Spain, and Latin America, do not play mere word and image games; they attempt instead to release material from layers of the mind that we normally hide from ourselves. American writers generally do not work in this way, though obviously some do. In poems like these two, however, it is much more likely that Ashbery is following the lead of such earlier American writers as Gertrude Stein and (less often) Wallace Stevens in choosing to play with technique rather than with reality or the truth.

Rather than being surrealistic, Ashbery is plugging in words and images that are admissible on technical grounds, but not on the basis of meaning. Thus syntax, language, and pure imagery determine the content of the poem, rendering it nonsensical. John Vernon has correctly said that Ashbery's humor "hovers between surrealism and a kind of epistemological skepticism, a refusal to mean or to respect meaning." He goes on to detail the rationale he assumes Ashbery is working under: "If we unpeel all the layers of language around us, tracing words back to their sources in other words, and still other words, what we find behind it all is not a 'world' or 'reality' or a presence of any kind, but simply an absence. . . . If there's a gap between words and things, then why not release words to play on their own, joke around, display themselves, invent, shuffle, entertain?" [19]

When used in short poems, such methods as these are instructive (on the possibilities of poetry) and entertaining (primarily for their disjunctive humor). Fragmentation, or discontinuity, is a far less attractive effect, however, in longer poems—where the accretion of significance through the use of consistent and repeated elements of form and meaning provides the coherence so essential to a reader's positive experience of the poem. As I have already suggested, Ashbery attends to these needs in his most successful long poem—one of the best of all his poems—"Self-Portrait in a Convex Mirror." Unfortunately, such poems as "Fantasia on 'The Nut-Brown Maid'" from *Houseboat Days* (1977) and "Litany" from *As We Know* (1979) are less successful. Perhaps it was in recognition of this fact that Ashbery chose to reprint so little of "Fantasia on 'The Nut-Brown Maid'" in his *Selected Poems*.

The case of the sixty-six page "Litany" is especially instructive. This work actually consists of two concurrent poems printed side by side, one in italic type. In a note, the author tells us that they are to be read as "simultaneous but independent monologues." We cannot read them simultaneously, and they do not form what we normally think of as a litany, in which one voice speaks, the other responds, and so on. Here we may want to imagine a kind of dialogue but are frustrated by the text; the two speakers never address one another directly; at most they seem to allude at times to the same objects—the weather at one point, for example, a photograph at another. Generally they do not even do that, preferring to talk to themselves rather than to each other or to us. As a result the reader feels lost in the middle of a world with isolated details but no connected landscape, a world that cannot be comprehended.

The poem does have several incidental surprises and charms to reward the diligent pilgrim. At one point, for example, the character using italics speaks eloquently about our time (or at least the time in which he lives) as the silver age—he describes its tenor, tells what kind of poets it needs, what critics. Elsewhere, the same character talks about a nice girl he met at the dog show, how he directed her to the ocean greyhounds. Toward the end we find a sudden series of sixteen lines all rhyming with the *ay* sound, this time spoken by the character using roman type. And so on. These moments are moderately entertaining, but they cannot make up for the rest of the poem, where one's frustrations grow along with one's impression that nothing here connects with anything else. A reader is left thinking that Ashbery's self-conscious experiments are better when conducted more briefly. None of this, however, is accidental; during my interview with him, Ashbery explained his motives for the poem: "I intended, in 'Litany,' to write something so utterly discursive that it would be beyond criticism — not because I wanted to punish critics, but because this would somehow exemplify the fullness, or, if you wish, the emptiness, of life, or, at any rate, its dimensionless quality. . . . The poem is of an immense length, and there is a lack of coherence between the parts."[20]

Whether "arbitrary" is one aspect of "dimensionless" might be debated; certainly one of the strongest effects of "Litany" is to illustrate the arbitrary, unpredictable, uncertain nature of our impressions of the world. In a short poem, we can be dazzled by Ashbery's inventiveness in presenting the arbitrary (the dimensionless, the simultaneously full and empty), by his verbal skill, his grammatical fireworks, and all his other wonders, and be done before frustration or exhaustion set in. But in "Litany," arbitrariness and absurdity are established and demonstrated at the very start when we still have sixty-five pages to go, sixty-five pages of arbitrary nonconversation conducted by two characters who seem to speak neither to one another nor to us — a disheartening prospect indeed. The further we read the less we have to hang on to, an effect precisely the opposite of what we find in most long poems.

In his devotion to the art-for-art's-sake aspects of poetry, Ashbery bears a stronger resemblance than any other poet discussed in this book to self-conscious practitioners of other arts, particularly painting, which he studied in his youth. "I have probably been influenced," he has said, "by the modern art that I have looked at. Certainly the simultaneity of cubism is something that has rubbed off on me, as well as the abstract expressionist idea that the work is a sort of record of its own coming into existence."[21] On another occasion

Ashbery further defined this latter point: "The process of writing poetry becomes the poem. This was radically demonstrated by action painters such as Jackson Pollock and Willem de Kooning, who set out not knowing where they were going, in a sensible trance, as it were, and created works of art which are themselves the histories of their own coming into being."[22] If the process of writing the poem itself becomes the poem, it is likely that the subject matter of such a poem will be poetry, and so it is in Ashbery's work.

The preoccupation with the art process as subject matter is a feature of all of Ashbery's books, but it especially dominates *Houseboat Days*, where he writes, in his most implicitly ironic gesture, almost exclusively about his own poems, the ones he is writing as he writes about them. The artist becomes his own theoretical critic, caught in the analytical lens even at the moment of conception. Interviewers of poets often ask the question, What gets you started on a poem — is it an idea, a theme, an image, a rhythm, or what? In "Variant," Ashbery not only answers the question — "Sometimes a word will start it," he says — but goes on to exemplify his doctrine. The unseen and unnamed interlocuter observes that "The way / Is fraught with danger"; Ashbery gratefully accepts the word and finishes the poem by writing around it:

I

Notice the word "fraught" as you are telling
Me about huge secret valleys some distance from
The mired fighting — "but always, lightly wooded
As they are, more deeply involved with the outcome
That will someday paste a black, bleeding label
In the sky, but until then
The echo, flowing freely in corridors, alleys,
And tame, surprised places far from anywhere,
Will be automatically locked out — *vox
Clamans* — do you see? End of tomorrow.
Don't try to start the car or look deeper
Into the eternal wimpling of the sky: luster

On luster, transparency floated onto the topmost layer
Until the whole thing overflows like a silver
Wedding cake or Christmas tree, in a cascade of tears."

It seems a pastoral poem, full of lovely images of an Edenic landscape, until we connect the "black, bleeding label" with the overflowing wedding cake, both floating in the sky, and realize that this is instead some kind of apocalyptic vision. Surely this is the sort of thing Ashbery was thinking of when he answered my question about his poetry being lighthearted by saying: "Some people wouldn't agree that my poetry is light-hearted. Frank O'Hara once said, 'I don't see why Kenneth likes John's work so much because he thinks everything should be funny and John's poetry is about as funny as a wrecked train.'"[23] And yet this poem has primarily to do neither with paradisal nature nor with apocalypse. It is instead a theoretical poem on the nature of language; it illustrates a "variant" on one's understanding of the word "fraught." While accomplishing this task, it also illustrates, in the fashion of an indirect ars poetica, Ashbery's poetic method.

As for what these poems say *about* poetry, they say that poetry can be whatever Ashbery wants it to be, and that this freedom or control may be applied not just to language but to the raw material supplied by the real world itself; it is, after all, a world of uncertainty. Ashbery agrees with Stevens that the imagination can do whatever it wants with reality, once reality has been taken into the poem. As Ashbery says at the beginning of "Collective Dawns": "You can have whatever you want, / . . . In the sense / Of twisting it to you, through long, spiralling afternoons." Of course it is also true that Ashbery, given his constant posing, his indulgence in false leads, occasionally claims to be a realist, a poet who wishes accurately to reproduce details of the real world, as he does in "The Explanation": "The orchestra is starting to tune up. / The tone-row of a dripping faucet is batted back and forth / Among the kitchen, the confusion outside, the pale bluster / Of the sky, the correct but insidious grass."[24]

But this is just a pose; Ashbery is even less a realist, less a literalist, than Stevens, as he makes abundantly clear in yet another of these poems on poetry:

It is argued that these structures address themselves
To exclusively aesthetic concerns, like windmills
On a vast plain. To which it is answered
That there are no other questions than these,
Half squashed in mud, emerging out of the moment
We all live, learning to like it.

The first two and a half lines echo a criticism often directed against Ashbery's poetry. The answer reiterates not just his artistic credo but also his attitude toward reality. In choosing an aesthetic approach to reality, Ashbery is asserting his artistic control over reality as something to be appropriated and ordered — or disordered — by the imagination.

Ashbery's most explicit poem about poetry, "What Is Poetry," also appears in *Houseboat Days*. It begins to answer the question posed in its title — without a question mark — by first offering a series of questions with question marks:

The medieval town, with frieze
Of boy scouts from Nagoya? The snow

That came when we wanted it to snow?
Beautiful images? Trying to avoid

Ideas, as in this poem? But we
Go back to them as to a wife, leaving

The mistress we desire? Now they
Will have to believe it

As we believe it. In school
All the thought got combed out:

What was left was like a field.
Shut your eyes, and you can feel it for miles around.

Now open them on a thin vertical path.
It might give us — what? — some flowers soon?

The first, complicated image is beautifully anachronistic, placing a representation of Japanese boy scouts within a medieval town; poetry has the power to do this. The second image similarly asserts the primacy of imagination. Matters become slightly more complicated when Ashbery turns his assertion that we go back from images to ideas into a question, away from the flat statement that the wording leads us to expect. The pronoun in the following statement is ambiguous; does "they" refer to readers and critics or to the ideas themselves, now personified? The statement after that is also mildly misleading; what Ashbery may mean is that school, by concentrating exclusively on the "thought" present in poetry, removed that element from one's future considerations of poetry, leaving to the speaker all other possibilities, including primarily the aesthetic ones. The poem ends with an assertion of these possibilities, telling us once again that poetry is free to do as it wishes with all the raw materials that reality presents to us — including, perhaps above all other possibilities, those that are most arbitrary and accidental.

In describing his composing practices, Ashbery often emphasizes their serendipitous aspects. His most extensive comment on this matter uses "What Is Poetry" for an example:

I often put in things that I have overheard people say, on the street for instance. Suddenly something fixes itself in the flow that is going on around one and seems to have a significance. In fact, there is an example of that in this poem, "What Is Poetry." In a bookstore I overheard a boy saying to a girl this last line: "It might give us—what?—some flowers soon?" I have no idea what the context was, but it suddenly seemed the way to end my poem. I am a believer in fortuitous accidents. . . . [and] it doesn't really matter so much what the individual thing is. Many times I will jot down ideas and phrases, and then when I am ready to write I can't find them. But it doesn't make any difference, because whatever comes along at that time will have the same quality. Whatever was there is replaceable. In fact, often in revising

I will remove the idea that was the original stimulus. I think I am more interested in the movement among ideas than in the ideas themselves, the way
one goes from one point to another rather than the destination or the
origin.[25]

One aim of Ashbery's method may be to illustrate the arbitrariness, the uncertainty, of reality itself; he will set up a situation at the start of the poem and then
deviate from it in an almost accidental fashion, using metaphor, indirection,
the wonders of syntax, unfettered imagination, things overheard on the street
or in a bookstore.

In his later work, however, beginning perhaps with the publication of *As We
Know* in 1979, Ashbery seems to address the question of meaning in a more direct and traditional way. Metaphor has always been one of his primary tools,
but rarely is it used to so clear an end as in "Flowering Death":

Ahead, starting from the far north, it wanders.
Its radish-strong gasoline fumes have probably been
Locked into your sinuses while you were away.
You will have to deliver it.
The flowers exist on the edge of breath, loose,
Having been laid there.
One gives pause to the other,
Or there will be a symmetry about their movements
Through which each is also an individual.

It is their collective blankness, however,
That betrays the notion of a thing not to be destroyed.
In this, how many facts we have fallen through
And still the old facade glimmers there,
A mirage, but permanent. We must first trick the idea
Into being, then dismantle it,
Scattering the pieces on the wind,
So that the old joy, modest as cake, as wine and friendship

Will stay with us at the last, backed by the night
Whose ruse gave it our final meaning.

The subject of the poem is dual, death and our reactions to it; the two are connected through the notion of smell. Wandering death is established as an especially powerful and caustic odor that has somehow become embedded in the sinuses of the poem's "you." The first stanza adopts the perspective so often used by Emily Dickinson, that of the dead or dying person, who also seems to notice the flowers that have been brought or sent. The two sources of odor compete with and complement one another at the end of the first stanza, leading us to the second, which switches to the perspective of the onlookers to this death. How shall they—we—respond? Curiously, what is most obvious to them is not the irrefutable fact of death itself, but the "mirage" that will not be destroyed, some comforting notion of the antideath, vague thoughts of eternal life. Thus the idea of death must be resurrected so that we can dismantle it with our consoling rituals.

Almost more than the subject of death, this poem is about our definitions of death and our responses to those definitions. The poem may be said, that is, to be more about our perception of reality than about that reality itself. The specific subject of perception comes even more substantially to the foreground in *A Wave*, which continues the growing commitment to coherent content that seems to have begun in *As We Know*. On the basis of these emphases, I would like to suggest that Ashbery can now be recognized as a philosophical poet, that indeed he has probably been this all along. I think he is such in two complementary senses. First, his growing interest in the largest and oldest questions of human life—love and death—makes him a philosopher of the quotidian. Second, his interest in the nature, functioning, and implications of human perception makes him a philosopher of epistemology: he wonders what we can know, how we can know it, how we can express it, and how our expression affects what we know. His conclusions on these matters make him very much a poet, perhaps the poet, of the age of uncertainty, the age of quantum physics.

The subjects of love and death, interestingly, seem to conflate in the poems in *A Wave*; we might say that the potential suitor, always on or just over the horizon, is the figure of Death. Though he appears in greater detail elsewhere, this suitor seems most completely defined in "They Like":

> At a corner you meet the one who makes you glad, like a stranger
> Off on some business. Come again soon. I will,
> I will. Only this time let your serious proposals stick out
> Into the bay a considerable distance, like piers. Remember
> I am not the stranger I seem to be, only casual
> And ruthless, but kind. Kind and strange. It isn't a warning.

Without quotation marks or some other system of signs we cannot know which statements are spoken by whom. Two impressions stand out, however. First, "love" in this book is always a new and casual meeting; it always seems to involve a new person, a stranger, rather than a stable situation, and that is unsettling. Second, the mingling of threat and attraction is also a consistent feature; the receiver of affection (essentially the central consciousness of the poems) does not know quite what to expect, though he is hopeful.

A similar sense of indeterminacy permeates the language of the book's title poem, which tries to tell the story of the meaning of life by placing this kind of love at its heart. Ashbery's notion of what life is seems to parallel the wave theory that is so integral to modern physics. For him, what is consistent in human life is not that kind of stable grounding, almost a kind of geography, that most of us seek, through which such things as love and death or joy and sorrow pass like waves. Rather, it is the principle of uncertainty, the principle of change, the energy wave itself that is most consistent in Ashbery's view of things. This underlying conviction is most clearly described in the long prose poem "Description of a Masque":

> Then we all realized what should have been obvious from the start: that the
> setting would go on evolving eternally, rolling its waves across our vision
> like an ocean, each one new yet recognizably a part of the same series,
> which was creation itself. Scenes from movies, plays, operas, television;
> decisive or little-known episodes from history; prenatal and other early

memories from our own solitary, separate pasts; events yet to come from life or art; calamities or moments of relaxation; universal or personal tragedies; or little vignettes from daily life that you just had to stop and laugh at, they were so funny, like the dog chasing its tail on the living-room rug. . . . And the corollary of all this was that we would go on witnessing these tableaux . . . there was no alternative to our interest in finding out what would happen next. . . . And event followed event according to an inner logic of its own.

The central passage of "A Wave," the one that seems to define the ground-level situation of the meditating character, is this ambiguous longing for love within the flux:

> What were the interruptions that
> Led us here and then shanghaied us if not sincere attempts to
> Understand and so desire another person, it doesn't
> Matter which one, and then, self-abandoned, to build ourselves
> So as to desire him fully, and at the last moment be
> Taken aback at such luck: the feeling, invisible but alert.

Having achieved his desire, the speaker suddenly fears it, is "Taken aback at such luck"; like a cornered animal he is alert to possibility and to danger. A similar indeterminacy shows itself in the language, again about love, that appears near the end of the poem: "But since you bring up the question / I will say I am not unhappy to place myself entirely / At your disposal temporarily."

Ashbery's most sustained expression of this complicated feeling occurs in one of the clearest poems in the book, "At North Farm," in which the suitor is an imminent possibility:

> Somewhere someone is traveling furiously toward you,
> At incredible speed, traveling day and night,
> Through blizzards and desert heat, across torrents, through narrow passes.
> But will he know where to find you,

Recognize you when he sees you,
Give you the thing he has for you?

Hardly anything grows here,
Yet the granaries are bursting with meal,
The sacks of meal piled to the rafters.
The streams run with sweetness, fattening fish;
Birds darken the sky. Is it enough
That the dish of milk is set out at night,
That we think of him sometimes,
Sometimes and always, with mixed feelings?

The feelings are mixed indeed. Though the oncomer is desired, his arrival is also prepared for with supplicating gestures rather than open arms. And the imagery used to describe him on his journey makes him sound more like a cruel avenger — death, in short — than a sweet lover. Still, he is desired and cannot be denied. Eros and Thanatos link arms on the road to the speaker of this poem.

In addition to being a philosophical poet generally, through his attentiveness to the nature of human life and the roles of love and death, Ashbery is a philosophical poet in the more special sense that he reflects in his poetry the way of seeing the world that is the basis of quantum physics. When he speaks of "our minds, parked in the sky over New York, / And nonetheless responsible," he is placing the creation of reality very much in the hands of human perception. As Shapiro has pointed out, "one of [Ashbery's] central themes is the breakdown of causality in the nineteenth-century sense. His discontinuities tend to throw us most clearly into the middle of the century of the Uncertainty Principle." [26]

Such understanding is found in many of the poems in *A Wave* — in "Cups with Broken Handles" and "Landscape" for example — though it appears most affectingly in "Down by the Station, Early in the Morning," probably because it is there conjoined with the subject of death. The poem begins by lamenting the gradual disintegration and disappearance of everything, including objects, gestures, sounds, the people associated with them:

It all wears out. I keep telling myself this, but
I can never believe me, though others do. Even things do.
And the things they do. Like the rasp of silk, or a certain
Glottal stop in your voice as you are telling me how you
Didn't have time to brush your teeth but gargled with Listerine
Instead. Each is a base one might wish to touch once more

Before dying. There's the moment years ago in the station in Venice,
The dark rainy afternoon in fourth grade, and the shoes then,
Made of a dull crinkled brown leather that no longer exists.
And nothing does, until you name it, remembering, and even then
It may not have existed, or existed only as a result
Of the perceptual dysfunction you've been carrying around for years.

The universe described here is one in which the observer does much of the creating; it is the universe of modern physics. Interestingly, Ashbery injects at the
end the notion of blame, as though this process were the creation of a dysfunc-
tional speaker rather than a true situation. In most poems, he would leave his
readers hanging after having done this; the poem would contain no evidence to
resolve the doubt. Indeed, he would most likely go on to an entirely new topic,
rendering this one unimportant. In this poem, however, he has already provided a solution. The answer appears in the first two lines, where the speaker is
unable to believe his perfectly obvious observation that things disintegrate —
which everyone else confirms. Thus we learn that the speaker is reliable in
everything but his understanding of himself; he is describing the nature of reality correctly, even when he says that memory is one way in which we create,
rather than remember, the world.

The rest of the poem deepens our understanding of this radically creative
process:

The result is magic, then terror, then pity at the emptiness,
Then air gradually bathing and filling the emptiness as it leaks,
Emoting all over something that is probably mere reportage

But nevertheless likes being emoted on. And so each day
Culminates in merriment as well as a deep shock like an electric one,

As the wrecking ball bursts through the wall with the bookshelves
Scattering the works of famous authors as well as those
Of more obscure ones, and books with no author, letting in
Space, and an extraneous babble from the street
Confirming the new value the hollow core has again, the light
From the lighthouse that protects as it pushes us away.

Every line here demonstrates the interpenetration that exists between the subjective and the objective worlds, the crucial importance of perception to Ashbery's way of understanding the world and writing poetry. The process described is one in which the world is constantly being destroyed and then re-created; each new vision of things becomes old and then is replaced. Fresh air floods in daily, causing both shock and freedom. The penultimate image, of the wrecking ball bursting through the bookshelves from behind, is particularly apt; with each infusion of new, creative air, the old creations are destroyed. What replaces them at first are the raw materials provided by the streets — and again we see Ashbery, walking out to overhear some random thing that will occupy the heart of his new vision.

Ashbery was once asked whether he drew consciously upon the insights of physics in constructing the universe of his poems: "Have you been specifically influenced in terms of a certain sense of indirectness, randomness, sense of time, by relativity, quantum mechanics or thermodynamics?" The poet began his answer by playing dumb; then he dropped a truer hint:

No, not at all, I know absolutely nothing about physics; I never took it in high school, I took chemistry instead. My maternal grandfather who had a great influence on my growing up was in fact a physicist and the head of the physics department at the University of Rochester so perhaps through osmosis some physics has come down to me.[27]

The answer, in other words, is yes; if we know anything about Ashbery's ways of thinking and knowing, it is that everything of importance comes to him through osmosis. The grandfather mentioned also happens to be the one with whom Ashbery lived during much of his childhood.

Thus there is a profound layer of meaning in Ashbery's poetry, but it occurs on a different level from what we will see in the work of the other poets treated here. Where most of them accept the truth of the world that they see, Ashbery is deeply suspicious of it, asking instead: how do I receive this truth and where does it reside? He is a doubter, profoundly uncertain about everything that he sees. His career may be said to travel from the almost indeterminate and meaningless chaos of his early experiments in style to a level where indeterminacy, uncertainty, chaos, and the participation of human perception in the essential nature of reality are his subject matter. In the final analysis, however, the two ways of seeing and doing are really one: Ashbery's view of the world has always been the way of modern physics; his goal has always been to study and to demonstrate the ways that art and the imagination participate in the creation of the world.

Finally, I would like to say just a word about my own methods in this essay. Early on I suggest that Ashbery's poetry is only about process and form, that it has no meaning in the traditional senses of the word. Many of my analyses of individual poems, however, search rigorously—and rather traditionally—for meaning, and—in my eyes at least—I seem to succeed. I hope that my readers, as they seek to understand this seeming contradiction, will refer themselves to the underlying thesis of this essay, the principle of uncertainty. I am convinced—certain—of the truth of everything that I say in this essay; but what I am most fundamentally saying is that truth is uncertain, in studying poetry as in studying the quantum world. Thus I am conscious of being a participant, a creator, of the truth that I perceive. I hope therefore, that no one will be surprised that my own method is based solidly—oh, very solidly indeed!—on the principle of uncertainty.

Stephen
Dobyns

The Uncertainties of Narrative

When he decided sometime before 1982 to write a series of poems based on the enigmatic paintings of twentieth-century French artist Balthus, Stephen Dobyns began a fertile investigation into the nature of poetry as an art form. Before he conceived and wrote *The Balthus Poems*, judging only from the results of his thinking, which are the poems themselves, Dobyns may well have been confused about the nature of his chosen medium; after *The Balthus Poems*, his understanding of his path seems to have clarified into allowing him to write his best and most distinctive poems. The key to the change is narrative, the way in which a writer chooses to manage time — for in poetry unlike in such art forms as painting and sculpture time is a powerful and necessary component. In a comment paraphrased by art critic Rosalind E. Krauss, Gotthold Lessing is reported to have said: "If the depiction of actions in time is natural to poetry, . . . it is not natural to sculpture or painting, for the character of the visual arts is that they are static." [1]

As *objects*, literary works are entirely symbolic; letters, syllables, words, are all visual renderings of sounds, themselves signs of meanings. When a literary work is physically beautiful, that is because of its extraliterary features — the typeface, the paper, the ink, the illustrations, the illuminations, whatever may be involved. Without these features, indeed, a literary work could hardly be called an object at all, even though in its written form it must be conveyed to the reader through the medium of an object. But this object is not the artwork itself; it is merely a thing that contains the artwork, as a box might contain a sculpture. Which is why Dottor Postiglione, the art restorer and lover in Robert Hellenga's novel *The Sixteen Pleasures*, says: "You can tear up a musical score without destroying the music. You can burn a novel without destroying the story. But a painting is itself, has no soul, no essence other than itself. It is what it is, a physical object. If it is destroyed, it is gone forever." [2]

As static objects, paintings and sculptures are relatively ineffective in presenting the movement of time; what they present instead are frozen moments that we may contemplate for as long as the artwork endures. Poems may not exactly give us objects that we can appreciate with our eyes, but they can give us effective renderings of actions taking place within time, actions that are perhaps used to make some point. In the case of Dobyns, this is what they give us, but only in his best, and later, work. In his earliest poems, Dobyns seems unaware of both the general power of narrative and his own particular talent at presenting it. In his first three books, Dobyns is primarily concerned with delivering various truths through discursiveness; rather than tell stories using concrete images he tends instead to use fantastic situations, generalized statements, and hazy speculations to arrive at puzzling but aphoristic conclusions. His early poems thus tend to be static, talky, and unreal, particularly when viewed from the perspective of the later, and much better, poems.

Dobyns does occasionally attempt to use narrative in his early poems, though generally in such an unreal and unbelievable way as to render them baffling and ineffective. "Passing the Word," which Dobyns presents as the first poem in the *Concurring Beasts* section of *Velocities: New and Selected Poems, 1966–1992* (1994), exhibits all these traits.[3] In the opening lines, Dobyns announces this poem as an ars poetica by defining

The poem as object; communicable; naked
as a mannequin after closing, stripped
between dressings, wig torn off, arms and legs

piled on the floor—the ability to rebuild,
a movement from nothing. The poem as bell
and the mannequin's head as clapper: a silent bell,
insistently proclaiming. Dogs stir. A cat
moves into shadow: now a jungle, now a tiger.

Had Dobyns stuck with his original image, the poem as mannequin, he might have been able to develop it to the point of successfully communicating meaning. But even at that earliest point in the poem, we do not know so many crucial things, primarily this: from whose perspective is the poem seen as a mannequin? The poet's? The reader's? That of the wife or husband of one of these two? Time is as mangled as the doll, being set first as "after closing" and then as "between dressings." Things get worse when the image of the poem mutates from being a mannequin to being a bell using "the mannequin's head as clapper." What does this mean? What does it mean when this bell becomes silent, though "insistently proclaiming"?

Narrative enters in the ninth line, where the poem, back to being a mannequin, appears "at your front door at three in the morning." Again we ask: at *whose* front door? Who is this character who "stumble[s] downstairs; a single slipper and slap / of bare foot; tugging at your robe" to greet "the mannequin dressed in dark silks— / a jumble of arms and legs for you to assemble"? Is it the poet meeting the poem he is going to write? Is it the reader of this (or perhaps any) mannequin poem, which must be assembled to be understood? Whoever this character is, his insubstantial identity begins to disintegrate as he attempts to deal with his visitor:

But you wait too long and now your face,
at best never more than tacked on, begins to slide,
drip like a bad tap between your slipper
and one bare foot. And you would move your arms,
legs, but suddenly they are moving into you,
into your body like sleeves turned inside out.

When a face begins to slide and leak, what does it become? Does Dobyns mean to suggest a penis? And when the arms and legs become inoperable and then collapse into the body, is the homeowner turning into the mannequin that he had earlier greeted on his doorstep? Is he becoming a turtle? Perhaps the best answer is, yes and no, both and neither.

Reading on, we learn that we need not worry about such questions as these; as the poem ends, Dobyns seems to take back most of what he has said:

> There is no harm here.
> You can refuse to accept it and in the morning
> it will be gone and you will have forgotten it,
> rearranged your face with a nail in the forehead.
> You will leave your front steps as it will have left
> the house you have opened to it and your wife with
> her half smile and dreams of trees heavy with apples.

The concluding lines seem to thrust us suddenly into the Garden of Eden, where the mannequin as Satan has seduced the housewife during the night. So poems are Satanic, and Adam (or is he Christ, with that nail in his forehead?) goes happily, though in a state of total confusion, off to work.

Perhaps because of a confused didactic impulse to say something undying about the art of poetry, Dobyns has muddled his images, his chronology, his story line, virtually everything he has touched. He communicates no intelligible lesson about poetry, no workable definition. Further, he has been exasperatingly coy about the identity of both his speaker and his central character, the *you* of the poem. Though we suspect that these characters may be one and the same person, we cannot be sure; and we cannot be sure what it would mean, were this true. Other poems in the early books are similarly unattractive, though sometimes perfectly clear. For example, in *Griffon* (1976), his second book, Dobyns has poems defining "Sloth," "Gluttony," "Anger," "Envy," "Covetousness," "Vanity," "Spite," "Bravado," "Absence," "Grief," and "Silence," in addition to a piece called "Six Poems on Moving," in which such characters as "A Shout," a "Wheel," "Rain," a "Sword," and an "Arrow" speak, reductively and literally, defining themselves. All in all, Dobyns' career as a poet had an unpromising beginning through his first three books.

One poem from *Heat Death* (1980), Dobyns' third book, does give some hint of the successful use he will make of narrative later in his career. Though still more argument than narrative, "The Body of Romulus" has the advantage of being an argument delivered through narrative. In fact the poem uses not one but two narrative lines, one more successfully than the other. Unfortunately, the less successful narrative is the one that governs the progress of the poem as a whole and its presentation of meaning. As the poem opens, the speaker describes how he and another person "stand on a hill above / Lake McBride" as "Beneath us several red snowmobiles / race across the ice." They stand there "For hours" and "argue about history," which the other person says "is simply the story of great names and ignores / those others who suffered to keep them fed." Though the speaker disagrees with this perspective, he is unable to formulate a convincing counterargument. "But later," he says, "in Plutarch I read of Romulus," and the story that he finds there is the one he uses to make his point — in absentia, as it were, from his antagonist.

It is this remembered story, delivered within the context of its surrounding story, that exhibits Dobyns' successful use of narrative in the poem. He tells us "how one day," Romulus was

> haranguing his people in a place called Goat's Marsh when a storm
> overtook the sky turning day to night and how people fled and the senators
> grouped together. When the storm passed, Romulus had disappeared and
> the senators claimed he had been lifted body and soul directly into heaven.
> One even swore he had seen Romulus taller and more beautiful than
> before, dressed in flaming armor, and that Romulus told him he was
> departing from Rome to become a god and henceforward he should be
> worshipped under the name of Quirinus. But Plutarch tells us that while
> the soul of a good man is like dry light which flies from the body as
> lightning breaks from a cloud, and while the soul of a wicked man rises
> from the body like heavy incense, it is wrong to think body and soul can

be transported together into heaven. Instead he argues that after Romulus won his battles and established his city he became as all men do who are raised by good fortune to greatness, that he gave up popular behavior for kingly arrogance, that he no longer maintained his office but dressed in scarlet with the purple-bordered robe over it and that he surrounded himself with young men with clubs who carried thongs of leather to bind up whomever Romulus commanded. And Plutarch suggests that when the sky turned black with terrible thunderings and boisterous winds from all quarters, and when people fled and the men with clubs fled, then the senators grouped around Romulus and slew him and cut up his body and each carried away a small piece in his bosom while rain carried away the blood.

Though these lines may seem like hacked up prose at first glance, in fact they are exemplary of the quiet lyricism found in much contemporary American free verse.

We might note first that though the lines are not metrically regular most of them contain five stressed syllables, and many of them contain interesting internal rhythmic patterns. For example, the third line quoted above, "how people fled and the senators grouped together," exhibits counterpoint first between the essentially dactyllic rhythm used through the four feet culminating with the syllable "group," and, second, between the trochaic rhythm that takes over beginning with that same syllable. Similar patterns exist in other lines as well. Reinforcing this rhythmic richness are such other techniques as simple repetition ("fled," "carried away"), alliteration ("body . . . bosom . . . blood"), consonance ("popular behavior . . . longer . . . scarlet with the purple-bordered robe over . . . surrounded"), near rhyme ("greatness" / "arrogance" / "dressed"), and a reliance on imagery ("dry light which flies from the body as lightning / breaks from a cloud") quite different from what we normally find in prose.

This is, in short, a well told story, exhibiting a level of narrative skill seen neither heretofore in Dobyns' work nor in the rest of this poem. After this passage, Dobyns returns to the dramatic situation with which the poem began. Unfortunately, however, that situation is no longer dramatic: the antagonists have long since parted from one another, and the speaker is forced to deliver his answer into the air or—more precisely—into this poem. And as if that were not unreal enough, the answer he delivers is so poetic, so romantic, as to be meaningless. In response to the notion that history "is simply the story of great names and ignores / those others who suffered to keep them fed," the speaker says that "although the great names of history are given words / in books, . . . / to all the others are given the body of Romulus." Thus, whenever a leader becomes a despot —"even here / in this small Iowa town where . . . sleep is an official sport"—

> even here the small names will trickle into the street like small drops of water, and with them they will carry tokens from the past: perfectly shaped fingers, bones, pieces of liver, the bright blue eyes of the god.

Surely these lines are excessively literary, excessively poetic. I refer not just to the repetition of the precious poetic notion of smallness, but also to the use of the word "perfectly." How could the pieces of Romulus' body remain "perfectly shaped" after being hacked apart in a great rush by the senators? Finally, the notion that these tiny, iconic emblems, these talismanic symbols, will trickle into the streets of this Iowa town and enlighten, with an appreciation of history, a bunch of people who spend most of their time sleeping is, to say the least, unconvincing.

Having written three books that fail because of their didacticism, Dobyns made a wise decision when he turned for his next project to the paintings of Balthus. Rather than try to impose meaning on these static works of art, he attempted to infuse them with action and narrative, imagining what happens either just before or just after the moment captured by the painter. As Gilbert Allen has noticed, "Dobyns is trying to extend moments into motion" in these poems.[4] The book contains thirty-two poems, each based upon a different painting, and a brief prefatory note in which Dobyns explains that the poems "are not intended to interpret the paintings or explain the intentions of the artist. Rather, I tried to turn each painting into a personal metaphor to create narrative poems seemingly free from the lyrical first person voice."[5]

An increased commitment to narrative is not the only refinement Dobyns achieves in *The Balthus Poems*; as this prefatory note shows, he now has a deeper interest in the role played by personality, specifically the personality of the poet, in poetry. Not that we really learn much about him; although the outlines of a personality do inevitably emerge from his books, Dobyns does not write autobiographical poems. Because of this his work has been condemned by some critics for being "over-controlled, hyper-understated, repetitious"; his "detachment" has been called "the major weakness in his poetry. . . . Dobyns' best work suffers from a lack of human warmth and feeling." Still, this very impersonality also happens to be one of the defining characteristics of Dobyns' poems. Thus other critics have praised the fact that, in his work, "one finds no easy confessionalism, few gratuitous details, no descriptions of nature connected by a vague mood of introspection. . . . The voice he employs is 'human' without being 'personal'; it is not overly impressed with its own sincerity."[6]

Verbally, the Balthus poems are not just "seemingly free from the lyrical first person voice," as the prefatory note promises; nowhere in them does Dobyns, or a created speaker, address us using the pronoun *I*. Instead Dobyns startles us as late as in the twenty-sixth of the thirty-two poems in the book by once again featuring the word *you*. This time, however, it is clear that he intends to use it to inject the creator's consciousness into his story: what had been a liability in the early poem "Passing the Word" now becomes an asset. The poem in which the word first appears, like the painting it is based on, is called "Katia Reading," and the second stanza begins: "All this is a painting you have seen often, and often / you have tried to determine what the girl is reading." The you is the viewer, but not just any viewer, not the reader— for, as the author also says in his preface: "my desire was to write poems that in no way would be dependent on a knowledge of the paintings or the artist." The viewer in question, then, can only be the poet, who takes this opportunity to explain the central importance of his own created world to his theory of art.

Looking more closely at the book in Katia's hands, he sees that it is "too thin for a novel; / and you have come to think it must be poetry." He then remembers "the first time / you read a poem that moved you," an experience that allowed—finally—for a transformation of the world:

> What had your world been until then? First you ate something, then you bought something, then you went bowling; a world where men passed their lives peering under the hoods of cars. And like the girl in the painting you must have turned your head slightly as if from a loud noise; and you too became like someone who has left on a journey, someone who has become the answer to his own impossible riddle: who condemned to his room is at last free of the room.

The result of this process is the poems in the book, all of which manage to break free of the "rooms" that contain them at the beginning, the paintings. They are equally free of the real world that may have inspired the paintings in the first place. By the time we arrive at either action or meaning in these poems, we have been removed from reality by at least two steps: first by the painting by Balthus, and second by the poem by Dobyns based on the painting by Balthus.

Such is the theory of these poems; their texture is considerably less dry. Dobyns generally begins with a quick, accurate description of the painting and then gradually adds life and imagination, as we can see in this middle passage from "The Greedy Child":

> A glass of white wine stands next to the bowl, while nearby the nearly full bottle is reflected in a baroque mirror with an ornate gilt frame. But the baby has no interest in the aesthetics of his surroundings. Instead he thrusts his hand toward the fruit as if the bowl itself might feel his desire and slide across the white marble, allow the baby to suck it in, bowl and all. Then he would tumble back, a round white heap, and with puckered lips he would try sucking the room toward him: he sucks and sucks until bits of paper begin fluttering through the air, until a gray hat rolls across the carpet, then a pair of felt slippers, until table and chairs crash to the floor, begin also to creep toward him.

Here Dobyns' method is revealed through his use of conditionality; his imagination takes over from that of the painter when he uses the phrase "as if." Beyond that point in the poem, he has left Balthus behind and is free to describe the spoiled babe in his own, in this case hyperbolic fashion. He creates, therefore, an uncertain world in which the future is not absolutely determined by the past. Further, the future of the situation is not inalterably inherent in itself; the observer participates in the experiment, as it were, helping to determine its outcome, much as the quantum physicist participates in the experiments that he or she conducts.

Most of the other poems in this volume create similar embellishments upon the paintings. In a small number of poems, however, something additional happens, something that indicates the core conception that fuses these pieces into a unified whole. I refer to the poems featuring Dobyns' "you" character, the poems that seem to act as ars poeticas because of the way they describe and develop the theory of poetry at use here. The most complicated (and the longest) of these is "The Passage"—based on Balthus' unusually crowded painting *Le passage du Commerce Saint André*—which concludes Dobyns' volume.

In the opening lines, the poet describes the central figures of the painting and enters the mind of one of them:

All this occurs at the intersection of two streets:
an old woman with a straw hat and black cane
approaches from the left, while with his back to you
a man wearing a blue sweater walks toward her.

The man is tall, erect and carries a loaf of bread.
He plans to pass through the doorway in front of him,
climb the stairs to a room where he'll eat lunch
and muse over the possibilities of his life to come.

It would strike him as inconceivable that he might
never pass the old woman.

We see here description, narrative, the building of suspense; in the painting it-self the man is young and strong, the woman old, deformed in the neck and shoulders. Dobyns finishes the tenth line above by asking a question that intro-duces the real subject of the poem: "Who knows that he won't?" (ever pass the old woman).

In the lines that follow, Dobyns continues his detailed description of the painting — and the development of his own narrative — by giving three nega-tive answers to this question, then a possible yes, then the first of two definite yeses. He also, toward the end of this passage, adds substance to his most important character, his "you":

> Not the fleecy white dog at his feet, nor the girl
> with a doll, nor the young woman behind her
>
> talking to a child in the window. Perhaps the man
> with a swollen face in a doorway at far left knows
> what will happen and that is why he stands back,
> refuses to take part in the activity of the street.
>
> Closest to you, standing in the street, a girl
> in a yellow blouse stares directly at you, holding
> her chin in her hand. She wants to see your face
> when the old woman touches the man with her cane,
>
> wants to see whether you respond with fear or
> mere incomprehension, thinking it must be some joke,
> as if the unfolding of the world were a story told
> for your amusement alone.

In the painting itself it is the girl in the yellow blouse who establishes the exis-tence of the "you," so intently does she stare from the canvas at someone we therefore know must be there: the viewer of the scene, the maker of the paint-ing, the author of the poem.

One other character in the scene is said to know what is about to happen, and it is through his perspective that Dobyns fills in the rest of his immediate story:

> Only the angular man
>
> sitting on the curb to your right seems indifferent
> to what will happen. Dressed in black, he looks like
> a retired juggler or acrobat. He saw the man pass
> carrying a loaf of bread, and knows you are watching,
>
> knows the man will meet his death at the intersection
> in front of the printing office, that he will stop
> as if struck by a sudden thought, look surprised
> as if struck by a sudden memory of his childhood,
>
> that he will drop the bread and sink to one knee.
> He knows the woman at the window will call out
> and the others will run to him, all except the girl
> in the yellow blouse who will continue to study your face.

Is this character, this prescient, retired juggler dressed in black, the figure of Death? Is he a Balthusian self-portrait? Certainly he is not the poet, whose photograph on the book's cover presents so distinctly different a visage — and of course we know (do we know?) that the poet occupies our viewing position, looking into the painting, about to be startled by its unpleasant turn of events, feeling unsettled by the relentless gaze of the girl in the yellow blouse.

As the poem ends, Dobyns completes his story while using the angular man to express the tenuous nature of human life:

> The angular man sees daily how people proceed through
> the city with their small anticipations such as simply

eating lunch or passing through a doorway, and it seems
to him that people move in elaborate shells like

the decorated shells of eggs, that each seems to see
his immediate future as a film played on the inside
of the shell; and in the imagined fulfillment of their
desires, each thinks of the present as already gone by.

The head of the man in the blue sweater is such a shell
as he proceeds toward a future he can almost touch,
unaware of the old woman with her shiny black purse,
not noticing how she lifts her cane as he approaches.

The angular man folds himself into himself, not wanting
to watch as the old woman stretches out her cane to touch
the eggshell head which like a shell cracks and breaks,
while the girl in the yellow blouse lifts her chin and smiles.

Neither the author nor the reader of this poem can emulate the choice made by
the angular man; we have to watch, and one of us has had to describe. Which
ignores the most important fact about this poem. In the painting the man in
the blue sweater is only walking down a street toward another street on which
an old woman approaches from his left. There is a girl in a yellow blouse (typical of all the girls in Balthus paintings, she is preternaturally wise, seeming to
know far more of human darkness than most of us will ever learn) and an angular man in black, but they like the rest of the characters are static, not moving. In short, the poet is the only person in this scenario with any ability to decide anything. The answer to the self-conscious question posed earlier in the
poem — "Who knows that he won't?" — is Stephen Dobyns himself; only the
poet knows at that point what will happen later in his poem. In a sly way that
deconstructs both the painting and the poem containing it, Dobyns makes his
choices.

Ultimately this poem is less concerned with the painting it describes than with questions of knowledge and foreknowledge, with the subject of human perception. The angular man thinks of people as being like eggshells, decorative on the outside while projecting films on the inside; what we know of ourselves, our pasts, presents, and futures, is what we cause to appear on the inside of those shells. In a sense, this poem may be understood as the film that Dobyns has chosen to project, for the moment, on the inside of his eggshell.[7] Indeed, so heavily are his poems determined, not by events taking place in the world of reality but by a speaker's perception and interpretation of those events, or imagined versions of them, that we could apply this notion to most of Dobyns' later work.

Thus Dobyns shares with Ashbery both an interest in the creativity of human perception and a sense of the uncertain, even arbitrary nature of the reality that they seem to inhabit and see. Although their poems are quite different in almost every other way, they are similar in this. The key to the connection is the perceiving consciousness of the poems, their heavy reliance on the personality of the characters who speak or dominate them. Of course, the two poets use speaking voices that are quite different. Ashbery mostly writes using the first-person mode of address, and his speaker is generally a naive, seemingly simpleminded character who has little notion of what is going on around him; he describes it and tries to make connections, but generally from a befuddled perspective: the poems tend toward humor because their speaker seems never quite to catch on. What he most importantly does not understand is that he does not understand; in most cases Ashbery's speaker is unable to analyze his own predicament. In contrast, when Dobyns writes in the first person his speaker is generally quite self-conscious; sometimes irritatingly self-conscious, sometimes amusingly self-conscious, sometimes depressively self-conscious. Of course, many of Dobyns' poems are not written — or seem not to be written — from a first-person perspective. Even these poems, however, have a speaker — representing perhaps the quintessential Dobyns poetic consciousness, speaker, or personality — and we will generally find him to be similar to the character sketched above.

The largest step forward that Dobyns takes in *The Balthus Poems*, the pivotal volume in his career, then, is in his increased use of narrative to structure his poems. The second largest step he takes is in his more subtle manipulation of self, personality, and speaking voice. In his following three books, the books that most fully define his achievement, Dobyns seems to consolidate his gains at the same time as he shifts his gaze back from the static world of the art object to the dynamic world of outward reality. He also takes a renewed interest in ordinary meaning: whereas the poems in *The Balthus Poems* are about themselves — investigating how description in art, replication, not only depends upon perception for its being, but is actually created by perception — the poems in *Black Dog, Red Dog, Cemetery Nights,* and *Body Traffic* return, this time skillfully, to the sorts of subjects that we found inexpertly handled in his early volumes.

Black Dog, Red Dog (1984), Dobyns' fifth individual collection, has poems that nicely illustrate three distinct patterns of feeling, thinking, perceiving, and therefore of narration, on the part of their speakers and central characters. The speaker of "General Matthei Drives Home Through Santiago," for example, follows a pattern quite similar to the one we have seen used in *The Balthus Poems.* The core of the poem is the speaker's description of a brief altercation that he witnessed; the bulk of the poem, however, is given over to his speculations about what may have happened before, around, during, and after this event. The speaker is quite self-conscious, like the speaker of *The Balthus Poems,* and the poem is chiefly about him, his perceptions, his thoughts, his hopes, and — ultimately — his political sympathies.

The poem is sixty-six lines long; verbal rhythm is achieved through the approximately five stresses and ten to fifteen syllables present in each line. It is also rhythmic in content, as Dobyns alternates passages in which his speaker is uncertain of what is or what has happened with passages in which he tells what he believes is true. Uncertainty dominates the poem both in terms of sheer volume, the number of lines devoted to it rather than to certainty, and in prominence, since the poem both begins and ends on notes of uncertainty. The reader is thus left with little doubt over which of these two conditions, certainty or uncertainty, is the more certain.

At the start of the poem, Dobyns' speaker tells us some of the things he does not know about the general:

The part where General Matthei leaves his office,
I don't know about. And when he gets home,
that I don't know about either. Or if he had
a hard day or an easy day or if his secretary
bent down in front of him so he could see her
large breasts or if he has a secretary or if she has breasts —
all this remains shrouded in mystery.

The lines are obviously focused upon the speaker, since the only certain information contained in them is his uncertain knowledge. It is, however, typical of
Dobyns in his later poems to render details, images, and events in clear and
certain terms, even when they are shrouded in uncertainty—and most of this
poem is shrouded in uncertainty. After a few more lines, in which the speaker
reveals several perhaps untrue details about the general's bowels, his wife's fi-
delity, and American cartoons on TV, he announces that "again the curtain of
mystery is lowered before us."

What the speaker does know about the general is that "for certain it takes
twelve men to help / General Matthei drive home; it takes five vehicles: / two
motorcycles with sirens and three big gray cars." He knows this from ordinary
observation ("the other generals of the Junta also rush home / at 100 kilome-
ters per hour down the crowded *avenidas*") and from what happened on this
particular occasion:

But yesterday as I was driving home and the general
was driving home and about a million other residents
of Santiago were also going home, I saw the small
humiliation of a middle-aged woman in a small red Fiat
who was neither beautiful, nor was she driving fast.

(We should note in passing that Dobyns, just as he uses alternation — pattern
and variation — in developing the overall structure of this poem, establishes
verbal rhythms by using repetition and variation in his phrasing, for example:
"driving home . . . driving home . . . going home," and "small / humiliation . . .

small red." The non sequitur in the last of these lines derives humor from the alternation pattern, through the use of "neither . . . nor.")

Later we are told of the exact incident that occasioned the writing of the poem:

> The military policeman riding the first motorcycle
> wore white leather gauntlets that nearly reached
> his elbows, and when the red Fiat had the audacity
> not to scramble for the curb, he swerved around it
> and smashed his fist down hard on the red Fiat's hood.
> For an instant, that was the loudest noise in Santiago.

The last line here is based not on fact but on speculation; thus it refocuses our attention on the speaker and on his awareness of what he does not know. As is true also in the poems of Charles Simic, politics here is the world of greatest uncertainty — and of greatest concern — for the speaker, just as it is the world that is able to act with the greatest certainty of its own.

Except for one more factual passage late in the poem — a romantic description of the blue sky and how "the lowering sun had just begun / to redden the tips of the snowcapped Andes" — everything else here is something the speaker can only guess about. This is true also, true especially we should perhaps say, of the political situation. To clarify this the speaker imagines late in the poem the possible reaction of the woman's husband to what has happened on her drive home. "Maybe," the speaker says, when the woman "told her husband about / the general . . . maybe he went out and stared at the Fiat / but saw nothing but a smear in the dust on the red hood." The lines are strikingly anticlimactic; what else could he have seen, we wonder?

Similarly, the concluding lines of the poem seem to promise a telling action, only to end with an imagined gesture:

> But maybe he looked at it and the rest of his family
> looked at it and maybe he mentioned it to some friends

and they looked at it too. And someday when General Matthei
is shot and dragged by his heels through the streets,
this man will think of his red Fiat and suck his teeth
and, in a way that is typical of the people of Santiago,
he will half roll and half shrug one of his shoulders
as if letting a heavy strap at last slide from it.

The first sentence here is conditional, uncertain; the key phrase is "But maybe." The second sentence, however, contains no speculation whatsoever; the speaker seems to know for certain that this is how the husband will react to the overthrow of General Matthei. That he reacts not with some triumphant gesture but with a half-shrug of one shoulder is our final indication of the speaker's political feeling and sophistication: though he does not care for the general, he knows that no meaningful changes will follow the general's overthrow. The poem is a carefully crafted narrative of the workings not so much of reality but of its speaker's mind as he observes, describes, and reacts to events that may have occurred in the real world.

The event that lies behind "All That Lies Buried"—from *Black Dog, Red Dog* but not reprinted in *Velocities*—may also have taken place in the real world, but it is so heavily colored by the speaker's obsession with his own dilemma and feelings that we get only the vaguest idea of what may have happened. The narration here is much more directly first person, since the speaker is also the primary actor in the poem. We meet this character as he is out walking at night amid falling snowflakes: "I catch several on my glove, / turn them over—blank on both sides. How / am I to continue with messages like these?" At first glance, the lines seem to have the speaker making fun of those who would seek understanding and personal guidance by interpreting signs from nature; soon enough we realize that he is serious. The speaker's approach is similar to that of Robert Penn Warren's speaker in "Code Book Lost," who knows that the truth is out there to be read, if only we knew the language: "Yes, message on message, like wind on water, in light or in dark, / The whole world pours at us. But the code book, somehow, is lost."

The speaker in Dobyns' poem has a problem; he seeks a message because of

> those harsh words I said tonight about
> separation and the loss of love — I see them now,
> little irregular lumps. And whatever hopes
> you had, my wife, they're out here too, those cold
> unweighables, buried deeper and deeper.

The best our speaker can do with the insights so far provided to him by nature is to create an analogy: both his actions and the "hopes" of his wife are mere lumps, like snowflakes. Having not found answers in the immediate world, the speaker decides to search the remnants of reality that inhabit his mind, his memory; he thinks of summer, of a bird he had watched some years ago, of the sea as it looked then:

> Sometimes a wave
> rushed in too fast, swamping the bird which
> then shook itself and continued, and I liked that,
> liked how the bird kept to the very edge.
> I even thought, that's the work I want for myself;
> as if that line were the division between world
> and soul — the place where life itself lies hidden.
> But tonight I think, isn't it living at the edge
> that makes the trouble — never getting comfortable
> or taking anything for granted, never trusting anything?

Although the source of the raw materials upon which understanding might be based has changed, the result is the same: ambiguity leads to doubt, doubt leads to uncertainty, uncertainty coupled with the current situation (the speaker's rudeness to his wife) leads to self-recrimination, and self-recrimination leads to depression while strengthening the speaker's feelings of doubt, ambiguity, and uncertainty.

Though he has failed twice in his quest for understanding, the speaker is not yet ready to give up; as the poem ends, he makes a final, desperate attempt to draw a lesson from his memory of the seashore:

What does the water leave at the wave's edge?
Whatever it leaves, the waves then hammer it down,
bury it deeper and deeper under the sand, as if
the wave's message, like the message of earth
or snow, is simply burial — the brain's message
to memory, the black dirt's message to a corpse.

"All That Lies Buried" thus ends, not with a solution to the problem posed by the speaker at the beginning, but with the speaker awash in depression; the only way out of his dilemma seems to be death, burial, corpsehood. Unlike that in "General Matthei Drives Home Through Santiago," this narrative has almost nothing to do with reality; the other character said to be involved is not even named, and we know nothing certain about their confrontation. The poem presents an excursion only through the disturbed thinking of the speaker.

The question of personality, the consciousness of the speaker or the poet, clearly lies at the heart of both of these poems from *Black Dog, Red Dog*, though in quite different ways. The speaker of "General Matthei Drives Home Through Santiago" is a hyperselfconscious storyteller; both involved in the incident and removed from it, he is objective and subjective at the same time, ever aware of his own perceptions and replications. The speaker of "All That Lies Buried," on the other hand, is entirely self-consumed, subjective to the point of being unaware of the reality of the world in which he lives. In a third poem from this book, "Wind Chimes," we find Dobyns using a third type of narration: the speaker seems so removed from the story he tells that we are almost seduced into thinking him an omniscient, third-person narrator. The poem has two long sections, each with thirty-four lines; the sections are separated by time — the two moments in time occupied by the central character — and by three dots placed at the end of the first section.

The writing in this poem is remarkable for its aura of precision, for the sense of accuracy that is apparent in its presentation of detail, for the patience of its pacing and movement. The readers' responses are carefully controlled, and the controlling agent is the poem's speaker, its narrator, its author. Dobyns seems to want to keep his distance from us in this poem, just as he seems to want to approach his subject matter from a great height. The only moment of artistic self-consciousness, the only time we feel the presence of the poet, occurs in the first two words of the poem, "Begin with," which draw our attention specifically to the speaker. After that, however, the poem seems to have the objectivity of a movie camera as Dobyns leisurely sets and circles in on his scene:

Begin with a Victorian cottage in a Rhode Island resort town — a two-story house of yellow shingles a block from the ocean with a roof like a Chinese pagoda and a screened-in porch on three sides. A wooden croquet set lies scattered on the lawn which is surrounded by a chest-high privet hedge. Hanging from the porch ceiling, a wind chimes with eight glass bars swings gently in a breeze smelling of salt and fried food from hot-dog stands along the beach.

The hedge forms a border that is penetrated only by the wind, which carries the smells up from the beach and causes the sounds produced by the wind chimes; though we feel, smell, and hear these things, we do not *see* anything outside of the grounds of the house.

Continuing his cinematic pan, Dobyns moves into the house, where "In the middle of the living room, / a boy lies on his stomach reading a Batman comic." (We almost expect him to be looking at a book of poems, like Katia in "Katia Reading" — in which case the central character of this poem would turn out to be the boy, tied to the narrator-poet through his interest in verse.) After additional description of the boy, who "slowly bumps his heels together as if in time / to the sound of the surf he hears in the distance" (another sound carried by the wind), Dobyns moves past a "dog panting at the foot of the stairs" to a bedroom upstairs, where

> a man lies naked on white sheets smoking a cigarette. His wife, also naked, sleeps with her head on his chest. As he smokes, the man carelessly strokes her back and stares up at the lines and angles of the white ceiling until it seems he's looking down from some high place, a plane or hilltop.

It is here that Dobyns draws a parallel between the elevated perspective of his narrator and the consciousness of the man, who is alone among the characters in the poem in being able to see something beyond the confines of this property: "he can just see / the roofs of other houses and he imagines his neighbors / drowsing their way through the August afternoon." This is the only thought he has here in the first section of the poem. Next, he watches his cigarette smoke "turn blue / as it rises through bars of sunlight to the ceiling," and he hears

> the sound of people
> playing tennis — an occasional shout and the plonk
> of the ball against the webbing of the racket;
> from the porch, he hears the tinkling of wind chimes
> like a miniature orchestra forever warming up.

Thus ends the first section of this poem, with a glance back at one of its opening images, the image of the title. The man is in a state of languid alertness as he experiences a defining moment in his life, a moment of particular emotional and sensual poignancy.

Or so it will seem "Years later," in the second section of the poem, when "the same man is lying fully clothed / on his bed in a city hotel . . . / waiting for a friend / and soon they will go out to dinner." The only light is from the street and from "a blinking / red sign outside his window." He again stares at the ceiling, and either that action or "some combination of sounds from the street" reminds him of the wind chimes. Much has changed in the intervening years—

His son is grown up; his wife has remarried.
He himself has a new wife in another city
and he's away from home only because of his work
in which he thinks himself happy and successful

— but suddenly, briefly, the man reinhabits his earlier life, relives that moment from the past: "he clearly hears the wind chimes, / sees the swaying curtains in that summer bedroom, / even feels the faint pressure of his ex-wife's / sleeping head upon his chest."

The memory is touching — to the reader, probably; to the man, certainly; and to the narrator, perhaps surprisingly, whose close bond to the man on the hotel bed is about to be revealed to us. Until this point the only thinker in this poem has been the narrator, whose mind and understanding have been everywhere. Now he is about to merge himself, his authorial perspective, his ability to think, with the consciousness of his central character, whom we see reflecting on "the complicated turnings of his life":

and he wonders if what he had seen as progress
was only a scrambling after circumstance, like a boy
trying to scramble into the back of a moving truck;
and while he doesn't regret his life, he grieves
for all that was lost, all that he had to let go.
He thinks of that ocean house and wishes he were back
in his former life or that one could take one moment
and remain inside it like an egg inside its shell,
instead of constantly being hurried into the future
by good luck or bad.

Ultimately, the desire to defeat time by achieving an eternal moment, expressed here by the man, is the desire of the poet — not just Dobyns, but any poet. What ties these lines, this thought, specifically to Dobyns is the reappearance of his eggshell image for this notion, which we saw used similarly in "The Passage." The handling of personality in this poem is as complex as it is discreet; Dobyns seems to place his own feelings at a considerable distance from himself, revealing his kinship with his central character only obliquely, and only near the end of the poem.

Which is not to say that the man in this poem *is* Stephen Dobyns, that the man's experience is one that Dobyns himself has had. What they share is nothing so mundane as this, but a feeling about the passage of time, a feeling that is expressed through the medium of narrative. Thus Dobyns shows himself to be something of a philosophical poet, a poet interested in the meanings of things. This concern comes even more to the fore in his next book, *Cemetery Nights* (1987), in which he tells a series of stories or narratives in the third person about characters who are puzzled by reality, puzzled by their lives, and searching for some way to understand these things, or at least some way to endure from day to day. Meanwhile, as the title of the book indicates, death awaits us at the end of the day, at the end of our life and our reality. The fact of death lends urgency to the situations of these poems, just as it robs them of meaning; Dobyns has a good bit of fun in this book with the mythologies of death — with its angels, its demons, its heaven and its hell — but true spirituality has little to do with his vision; ultimately, he views both life and death in strictly timebound and physical terms.

Generally, Dobyns is much more an author of individual poems than a developer of integrated sequences, an architect of cohesive books. *The Balthus Poems* is an exception of sorts, however, and so is *Cemetery Nights*. Several of the poems are about the realm of the dead, in particular the five title poems scattered throughout the volume and distinguished from one another by their Roman numerals. The rest of the poems are about life, but life lived in anticipation of death and, therefore, life lived with a hungering for meaning. The key poem from this philosophical perspective is "Spider Web," which Dobyns delivers from the lofty third-person point of view that he has come to favor. The poem begins with a thesis statement:

There are stories that unwind themselves as simply
as a ball of string. A man is on a plane between
New York and Denver. He sees his life

as moving along a straight line. Today here,
tomorrow there. The destination is not so
important as the progression itself.

The narration of this poem, the way it handles time, is strictly and traditionally
linear; the action moves forward in a straight line. Meaning, too, is handled
traditionally, by forming a kind of circle: at the end, the poem reaches back to
the beginning to answer the question that was implicitly posed then. This answer, as we shall see, offers another possible pattern, in which a distressingly
fluid and defenseless combination of semicircular lines makes an implicit
philosophical statement.

Over lunch during his flight, the man chats with the woman seated next
to him, a woman whose life has been dominated by a devastating pair of accidents: "It turns out she has had two children killed / by drunk drivers, two
incidents fifteen / years apart." Her reaction is about what one would expect:

> At first I wanted to die every day,
> she says, now I only want to die now and then.
> Again and again, she tries to make her life
> move forward in a straight line but it keeps
> curving back to those two deaths, curves back
> like a fishhook stuck through her gut.

Her conversation curves back similarly; though the two of them go on to talk
about other subjects, she keeps coming back to this one. And so does he, after
they part: during his business meetings, over dinner, he keeps telling people
about her and her story, keeps trying to "describe / how the woman herself
fought to keep the subject / straight, keep it from bending back to the fact / of
the dead children." She keeps laying down straight lines, only to have them
bend back in circles upon her.

After about a week, the man returns home and "gathers up the threads of
his life." As he works in his garden and repairs things in the house,

He thinks of how a spider makes its web;
how the web is torn by people with brooms,
insects, rapacious birds; how the spider
rebuilds and rebuilds, until the wind
takes the web and breaks it and flicks it
into heaven's blue and innocent immensity.

No longer does the man see "his life / as moving along a straight line"; nor is he able to circle neatly back to the settled view of life that he had at the beginning of this poem (though the pattern of the poem itself does exactly that). As in James Wright's poem, "The Journey," life is now seen as having the pattern and durability of a spiderweb: it is confusing; it is everchanging; it is shortlasting; it is subject to the destructive whims of an uncaring and "innocent" universe. The speaker's perspective on "heaven" is unknowing, distanced to the point of alienation, and ironic. Dobyns seems to view both the idea of a spiritual other-world and the notion of divinity as cosmic delusions perpetrated by men upon man or by a man upon himself.

Many of these poems are so broadly comic on their surfaces that it is almost possible to miss the despair that seems to lurk beneath that level. The title "How to Like It," for example, makes the poem sound like it will be a sort of guide to enjoying life; only at the end does the phrase turn into a question that implies ultimate human meaninglessness. The poem is narrative and presented from the third-person point of view; it has two main characters almost equal in importance — a man and his dog — though the mood that dominates the poem is definitely that of the man: once again the anonymous male protagonist of a Dobyns poem is seen embodying and enacting the speaker's thoughts, and authorial distance shrinks to nothingness.

The opening five lines establish a mood as though from nowhere, an observation on the changing of the seasons:

These are the first days of fall. The wind
at evening smells of roads still to be traveled,

while the sound of leaves blowing across the lawns
is like an unsettled feeling in the blood,
the desire to get in a car and just keep driving.

Who smells this wind, hears these leaves, has this feeling in the blood, this desire to escape? Why, it is both "A man and his dog," who, in the next line, "descend their front steps" together. Immediately we learn that they have different agendas, different escapes in mind:

The dog says, Let's go downtown and get crazy drunk.
Let's tip over all the trash cans we can find.
This is how dogs deal with the prospect of change.
But in his sense of the season, the man is struck
by the oppressiveness of his past, how his memories
which were shifting and fluid have grown more solid
until it seems he can see remembered faces
caught up among the dark places in the trees.

The dog is like the unrestrained id of the man's adolescence, eager for action, while the man himself is moony, broody, unhappily nostalgic, scarcely able to move beneath the weight of his thoughts.[8] Indeed, he sounds a lot like the disembodied narrator who defined the seasons at the start of the poem.

This pattern of alternation continues throughout the poem. When the dog wants to "pick up some girls and just / rip off their clothes," the man "notices wisps of cloud / crossing the face of the moon" and yearns to begin his lonely journey; when the dog wants to "go down to the diner and sniff / people's legs," the man imagines a "road" that is "empty and dark." Eventually, the dog begins to absorb the man's mood and suggests that they just "go to sleep. Let's lie down / by the fire and put our tails over our noses." When the man continues his dream of escape, of a solitary journey, the dog seems to become even more discouraged and suggests: "Let's just go back inside. / Let's not do anything tonight." The poem ends:

                              So they
walk back up the sidewalk to the front steps.
How is it possible to want so many things
and still want nothing? The man wants to sleep
and wants to hit his head again and again
against a wall. Why is it all so difficult?
But the dog says, Let's go make a sandwich.
Let's make the tallest sandwich anyone's ever seen.
And that's what they do and that's where the man's
wife finds him, staring into the refrigerator
as if into the place where the answers are kept —
the ones telling why you get up in the morning
and how it is possible to sleep at night,
answers to what comes next and how to like it.

Everything is difficult for the man, nothing is difficult for the dog — but at least here, for once, they seem to agree about something: the necessity of a late-night sandwich. Though the lines are amusing on the surface, the despair the man feels at the utter meaninglessness of his life is not amusing. Least amusing of all, perhaps, is what happens with the narrative voice, which brings together the outlooks of the man and the author. It is impossible not to think that the man's sense of sad ennui expresses the feelings of the poet. The title gradually loses its seeming imperativeness throughout the poem; it ends up being the most plaintive question of all: How are we to like what comes next in our lives?

What inevitably comes next for the man, for the author, for the empathetic reader, for everyone, is another step along the path of time, another step toward death, toward the cemetery nights of the book's title. In the five separate poems having that title (four of which are reprinted in *Velocities*), we seem to see what Dobyns the philosophical poet really thinks about the ultimate significance of human life. The first of these poems, the one that opens the book, has two stanzas, the second of which provides a commentary on the first. The poem has a kind of thesis, given by our apparently omniscient narrator in the first two lines: "Sweet dreams, sweet memories, sweet taste of earth: / here's how the dead pretend they're still alive." There follow four illustrations, each of which has the same pattern:

> Two of the dead roll on the ground,
> banging and rubbing their bodies together
> as if in love or frenzy. No matter if their skin
> breaks off, that their genitals are just a memory.

The dead are apparently soulless; in other poems we learn that they are invisible to the living and that they fade away gradually, as their bodies decompose: once a body has turned completely to dust, then the person is utterly dead.

Until then, these dead people attempt to continue the lives they formerly led — futilely and, in the eyes of the rats introduced in the second stanza, hilariously:

> The head cemetery rat calls in all the city rats,
> who pay him what rats find valuable —
> the wing of a pigeon or ear of a dog.
> The rats perch on tombstones and the cheap
> statues of angels and, oh, they hold their bellies
> and laugh, laugh until their guts half break;
> while the stars give off the same cold light
> that all these dead once planned their lives by,
> and in someone's yard a dog barks and barks
> just to see if some animal as dumb as he is
> will wake from sleep and perhaps bark back.

Rats are smart in these poems, and dogs are dumb; dead human beings are even dumber than dogs. Living human beings can be relatively smart about everyday things, but — as we have just seen in "How to Like It" — they are always sadly stupid when it comes to meanings, patterns, plans, the significance of it all. The authorial speaker of "Cemetery Nights," meanwhile, is smart about both the living and the dead, about the futility of their endeavors. Unfortunately, his perspective is echoed more by the rats than by any of the other characters in this poem.

Though the humor of this poem is cynical to the point of being caustic, at least the poem does benefit from humor; much darker is "Cemetery Nights V," which concludes the volume. In the first stanza the speaker pictures the realm of the dead in terms of an ancient mystic symbol, an enormous, cosmos-spanning wheel of fire:

> Wheel of memory, wheel of forgetting, bitter
> taste in the mouth — those who have been dead longest
> group together in the center of the graveyard
> facing inward. The sooner they become dust the better.
> They pick at their flesh and watch it crumble,
> they chip at their bones and watch them dissolve.
> Do they have memories? Just shadows in the mind
> like a hand passing between a candle and a wall.
> Those who have been dead a lesser time stand
> closer to the fence, but already they have started
> turning away. Maybe they still have some sadness.
> And what are their thoughts? Colors mostly,
> sunset, sunrise, a burning house, someone waving
> from the flames. Those who have recently died
> line up against the fence facing outward,
> watching the mailman, deliverymen, the children
> returning from school, listening to the church bells
> dealing out the hours of the living day.
> So arranged, the dead form a great spoked wheel —
> such is the fiery wheel that rolls through heaven.

This speaker addresses us from a vast, elevated distance; his definition of and commentary on the dead adopts not just the stance of Old Testament prophets, but their vocabulary and tone as well. We see here the Dobyns narrator, the Dobyns authorial voice, in its most philosophical, its most didactic, its most hopeless and despairing phase.

In the second and concluding stanza of this poem, Dobyns gradually focuses in on a lone member of the newly dead:

> For the rats, nothing is more ridiculous
> than the recently dead as they press against
> the railing with their arms stuck between the bars.
> Occasionally, one sees a friend, even a loved one.
> Then what a shouting takes place as the dead
> tries to catch the eye of the living. One actually
> sees his wife waiting for a bus and he reaches out
> so close that he nearly touches her yellow hair.
> During life they were great lovers. Maybe
> he should throw a finger at her, something
> to attract her attention. Like a scarecrow
> in a stiff wind, the dead husband waves his arms.

The lines are familiar in many ways, as we again meet our friends, the grave-yard rats, and we see again (in the image of that finger) Dobyns' penchant for slapstick humor. More importantly, we again encounter a central character who is not only a man but a husband; and not just any husband but a lonely one, far from home, unable to reach the one he loves.

After these lines, Dobyns turns his attention from the husband to the wife, as the husband frantically waves at her. The speaker wonders:

> Is she aware of anything? Perhaps a slight breeze
> on an otherwise still day, perhaps a smell of earth.
> And what does she remember? Sometimes, when
> she sits in his favorite chair or drinks a wine
> that he liked, she will recall his face but
> much faded, like a favorite dress washed too often.

As we will see more emphatically soon, the wife has moved foward since her husband's death, leaving the past behind while he is still stuck in that last moment, pining for her. And though this may seem like just one isolated instance of man-woman relations, it follows a pattern generally present in Dobyns' poems, where women seem present only as shadows or pawns. Though we often get inside the heads and minds of Dobyns' men characters, we never get inside those of his women characters. Women are mysterious, unemotional, uncaring, perhaps even selfish in the lives of Dobyns' men, for we see the women only through these men's eyes. Meanwhile, Dobyns' men often suffer from a crippling sense of nostalgia, as is the case with the corpse in "Cemetery Nights V": "And her husband, what does he think? As a piece / of crumpled paper burns within a fire, / so the thought of her burns within his brain."

Immediately after these lines the poem ends by returning to the woman, to the perspective of the living, to their attitude toward their own lives and toward the dead:

> And where is she going? These days she has taken
> a new lover and she's going to his apartment. Even
> as she waits, she sees herself sitting on his bed
> as he unfastens the buttons of her blouse.
> He will cup her breasts in his hands. A sudden
> breeze will invade the room, making the dust
> motes dance and sparkle as if each bright
> spot were a single sharp-eyed intelligence,
> as if the vast legion of the dead had come
> with their unbearable jumble of envy and regret
> to watch the man as he drops his head,
> presses his mouth to the erect nipple.

The passage before this one begins, "And her husband, what does he think?"; this one begins, "And where is she going?" The difference could hardly be greater; the implications could hardly be clearer: the woman is given no feelings, not for her dead husband and not for the lover who is pawing on her now.

She merely watches him paw, much as the cold, aloof speaker seems to watch his characters as they perform in the poems.

There is, however, one significant difference: while we have been able to ferret out the feelings and thoughts of the speaker—by following how he identifies his perspective with that of his male protagonists—we cannot ferret out this woman's thoughts and feelings. She seems not to have any; Dobyns will not, seemingly cannot, echo what is in her mind. Even in these lines supposedly devoted to her, all of the thinking, acting, and reacting comes from the man in the poem. It is he who unbuttons her blouse; he who cups her breasts; he who kisses her nipple—and he alone who feels the presence of the dead in the dust motes that invade the room. The speaker can identify with the man but not with the woman, just as he was able to identify with the dead husband earlier in the poem, and with a whole long series of similar men in other poems.

And what a bunch they are, all of them so much like one another, all of them so similar to the speaker of the poems in which they appear. Although Dobyns has written of a great many characters and situations during his career, more recently he has been concentrating on the lives and thoughts of these confused, depressed, middle-aged, representative American men. *Cemetery Nights* deals with these characters as they anticipate, react to, and begin to inhabit the realm of death. The book that follows, *Body Traffic* (1990), similarly deals with questions about the human body, including its relationship to the person (the man) who inhabits it. I am going to conclude my discussion of Stephen Dobyns by looking at just one poem from this book—"Toting It Up," which may have been intended as a final commentary on this representative character. The other poems in *Body Traffic* are similar enough in both style and content to the poems in *Cemetery Nights* that I do not feel a need to comment on them. I am also not going to discuss any of the eighteen new poems published in *Velocities* in 1994, though for a different reason: these poems seem merely anecdotal to me, a series of superficial stories with no thematic depth.

"Toting It Up" is a simple poem, a seven-stanza, twenty-one-line tour-de-force summary of one futile, meaningless life:

He bought one pair of boots, then another.
They were good boots. He had a four boots life.
He bought twelve cars. He had a twelve car life.

He had fifty-three hundred orgasms but hungered
for a few hundred more. He had two wives:
a two wife life, a four kids life, a twelve

grandchildren life. He drank thirty-four thousand
six hundred and sixty-six cups of coffee.
He ate a quarter of a ton of spaghetti.

He had five heart attacks: a five heart attack life.
He was in the hospital ten times. He had
a two cane life, a one pair of crutches life,

a one wheelchair life, a one final illness life,
and all his memories vanished like bubbles
from a glass of champagne. His last suit of clothes

turned to dust and his coffin turned to dust
more slowly. To his grandchildren he was a face,
to their children a name, and to their children

a vacancy, and over his grave a road was built,
and the world rolled down that road. See there
in the distance, that brightly disappearing speck.

The poem is very much representative of Dobyns' "philosophical" thinking generally: not only is the individual life utterly insignificant, composed as it is of trivial details, but the entire "world"—by which Dobyns certainly means the whole waxball of human existence, including its triumphs and tragedies, its culture and chaos, its arts and its sciences, its good deeds and evil, its whole long history and its momentary existence — is meaningless as well.

And yet the poem is funny, as Dobyns' poems so often are. Some of the humor comes from the wry way this philosophy is expressed; some of it also comes from the form taken by the narrative. Earlier, while discussing the poem "Spider Web," I suggested the existence of a fertile narrative tension between patterns of linearity and circularity in Dobyns' poems. In this poem we see another pattern — one that Dobyns also uses with some frequency— in which linearity is taken to an extreme and the poem is not allowed to circle back to the start, neither to enrich its character nor to tie its thesis or its message into a neat, circular knot. Still, poems written in this form do not give the reader an impression of discontinuity; the meanings do seem both consonant with the form and, somehow, circularly related to the events and images of the poems. Thus in "Toting It Up," both meaning and form express, through their runaway linearity, the meaninglessness and insubstantiality not just of human life, but of all existence as well.

As I have said, humor mostly exists on the surface of Dobyns' poems; when we go deeper, things are quite different from funny. Speaking of the humor in Dobyns' first book, *Concurring Beasts* (1972), Peter Cooley suggests that the poet "has a dry wit which succeeds in winking at the surprising even within the texture of poems where the unexpected is his norm."[9] This is true of the earlier work; later, however, Dobyns' sense of the unexpected becomes too serious for him merely to wink at it. This development goes along with the poet's deepening understanding of the nature of his world, a world quite similar to the one inhabited by Ashbery, which is "a world," in the words of Richard Jackson, "where the relationship between discourse and order, words and things, has already begun to disintegrate. What [Dobyns] must deal with, then, as he says in a poem on the loss of a friend's daughter, are 'fragments of language, / fragments of blue sky.'"[10] Thus the humor in Dobyns' most mature, most serious poems is only skin deep. After a long look at Dobyns' career, it is hard not to agree with Mary Kinzie's comment on the knife imagery that is so predominant in *Griffon*, Dobyns' second book of poems: "I offer the following hypothesis: that the poems in *Griffon* are all part of a long kenning designed to keep the hand away from the knife. . . . Violence, and especially that of psychological dislocation . . . , is the ruling spirit of the book. . . . Laughter in the teeth of one's own grimace is one of life's great humiliations; Dobyns records it fearfully and well."[11]

Certainly Dobyns and the characters in his poems inhabit a world of uncertainty. But where Ashbery seems able to accept the nature of this world and see the absurdity occupying its heart, Dobyns seems to long for a more orderly, more meaningful, more predictable, more fulfilling world. Thus, where Ashbery reacts to the contemporary world with good humor, Dobyns ultimately reacts to it with depression, veiled despair. Though he tries heroically to know "what comes next, and how to like it," he fails in both regards: in a world of uncertainty, he cannot ever know what is going to come next, and he always seems to expect the worst. Of course he never learns to like it, however much he may seem to enjoy some parts of the journey.

Charles
Simic

Poetry in a Time of Madness

Charles Simic's *Selected Poems, 1963–1983*, first published in 1985 and then again in 1990 in a "Revised and Expanded" form, is unusual, not just because of this publishing history, and not just because it did not win a Pulitzer Prize in its first version (in a year with little serious competition), but also because it is cumulatively superior as a collection to the parts that went into its making. Like William Stafford, Simic seems a relatively casual poet; he seems to toss his poems off as the spirit moves him, with no larger plan in mind than the impulse at hand. When the time comes for a book, it seems that he gathers the poems that he has on hand, puts them into a reasonable order that may (or may not) reflect some vague idea, and offers up the collection for publication.

Many of Simic's book titles reflect the relative randomness of their structures, such as *Classic Ballroom Dances*, *Weather Forecast for Utopia and Vicinity*, and *Hotel Insomnia*. Other titles seem to indicate a more specific range of content—*Charon's Cosmology*, *Austerities*, *The World Doesn't End*, and *The Book of Gods and Devils*—though in fact each of these topics seems to come up in all of Simic's books while not being covered to any unusual degree in the book having the topic-title. Only two of Simic's major volumes—*Dismantling the Silence* and *Unending Blues*—have discernable thematic patterns, both of them vague and ironic: in the earlier volume, Simic seems to deconstruct the world until *only* silence is left, while in the later volume he seems to chronicle an end to the blues. Given the pervasiveness of Simic's commitment to randomness — the randomness of an uncertain world — critics wisely look to individual poems for an indication of the poet's deepest concerns, rather than to entire volumes.

Some of Simic's poems are more worthy of attention than others; what makes his selected volume superior to his other collections is that it includes only his better poems, omitting those that are slighter or merely funny. In these better poems we find a dense mingling of seriousness and humor; Simic does want to be funny, but he also wants to be serious, particularly when writing on political subjects. And he has another, still deeper aim: his powerful sense of love for the objects of this world makes him feel that they are somehow connected, that a tissue of unity underlies the chaotic surface variety that we see and hear. As I will explain later, Simic thinks the key to this level of unity lies in the agency of metaphor.

Because of his sense of humor, and because of the oddness of his images and metaphors, Simic has often been called a surrealist by critics, particularly those writing about his earlier and more jokey poems. In truth, however, "Simic has rarely settled for the Jungian ahistoricity typical of American period surrealism. Instead, [his] images — pre-industrial and 'archetypal' at first, distinctly urban and modern later on — bear the scars of historical witness." Beneath the occasionally surrealist surfaces of his poems, Simic is one of the fiercest realists writing today. As Steven Cramer goes on to say, "The eye of [his] early poems may be directed inward, but out of its corner we often see men about to be hanged."[1]

Simic's fundamental commitment to realism is clearly evident in a poem that appears in *The Book of Gods and Devils* (1990), one of the volumes published since the issuance of his *Selected Poems*. "A Letter" opens with the expression of a dilemma:

Dear philosophers, I get sad when I think.
Is it the same with you?

Just as I'm about to sink my teeth into the noumenon,
Some old girlfriend comes to distract me.
"She's not even alive!" I yell to the skies.

Thinking brings sadness to the speaker, apparently for two reasons: first because of his inability to grasp the noumenon (according to Kant, an "object" reached by intellectual intuition, without the aid of the senses), and second because of the nature of the objects that his thinking does allow him to come up with, in this case some old, dead "girlfriend."

The second stanza attempts to explain the process that the speaker's mind has followed:

The wintry light made me go that way.
I saw beds covered with identical gray blankets.
I saw grim-looking men holding a naked woman
While they hosed her with cold water.
Was that to calm her nerves, or was it punishment?

The speaker's thinking begins not within the process favored by Kant, "intellectual intuition," but with an ordinary sense impression; the mood of winter and its absence of color then call up his vision of a woman being tortured. Is this image, we wonder, a memory based upon an earlier sense impression, or a "noumenon" created through a violation of the process prescribed by Kant? It does not matter how we answer this question, for in either case Simic is rejecting Kant's own rejection (in this particular instance) of the world of actual things.

In the third and fourth stanzas of the poem, Simic essentially repeats, through another, parallel adventure, the philosophical argument his speaker is having with Kant:

I went to visit my friend Bob who said to me:
"We reach the real by overcoming the seduction of images."
I was overjoyed, until I realized

Such abstinence will never be possible for me.
I caught myself looking out the window.

Bob's father was taking their dog for a walk.
He moved with pain; the dog waited for him.
There was no one else in the park,
Only bare trees with an infinity of tragic shapes
To make thinking difficult.

Bob's words reflect the thinking of Kant, and Simic's speaker is at first ecstatic to receive this philosophical guidance. Immediately, however, the real world reasserts its primacy and the speaker realizes he cannot escape it, no matter how hard he tries. What is most interesting in this poem is what the speaker sees when he looks at the real world or what he envisions when he wanders in the realm of memory. Thinking of a past love, he focuses not on her soft breasts and honeyed parts but on her death; this leads him to imagine an institutionalized woman whose naked body is being hosed by cruel orderlies. Similarly, when he looks at the trees in a park, he sees "an infinity of tragic shapes." As is so often the case with Simic, the poem (like each of its stories) begins pleasantly enough, then turns vaguely horrifying.

As for the philosophical argument in this poem, the point is not that Simic does not think in his poems; he thinks a very great deal in them. But he bases his thinking on his seeing, and what he sees and has seen of the world often leads him to tragic and terrifying thoughts, many of them based on his view of history. It happens that the critics who have called Simic's work surrealistic are American critics. Often what seems surrealistic in the poems is the material most deeply reflective of Simic's eastern European heritage. At first glance the lines in many of his poems might appear nonsensical to an American reader, discontinuous, even illogical. An example is this passage from "Chorus for One Voice," first published in *Dismantling the Silence* (1971):

A sound of wings doesn't mean there's a bird.
If you've eaten today, no reason to think you'll eat tomorrow.

People can also be processed into soap.
The trees rustle. There's not always someone to answer them.
Moon hound of the north you come barking you come barking.
It's not only its own life that man's body has to endure.

Although the form of this stanza is indeed discontinuous, particularly to American eyes, a reader familiar with the nature of life in Europe during the Second World War would find these details almost too familiar, too closely related to one another. Lines two, three, and six refer respectively to hunger, the Holocaust, and torture; the rest of the passage reveals the emptiness, within such a context, of various mythological panaceas. The wings in line one suggest not some succoring spirit but the black angel of death; line four might refer to the absence of the wood sylphs so valued by poets like James Wright; and line five seems to give new life to the darker implications of Francis Thompson's *Hound of Heaven.*

Simic was born in Yugoslavia in 1938 and came to the United States at the age of sixteen, in 1954. He grew up in Belgrade and in the countryside surrounding it during the Second World War. As Vernon Young has pointed out, this fact of personal history, coupled with an attention to history generally, is an important component of his poetry: "Simic, a Yugoslav, born to gallows humour as the sparks fly upward, is hounded by the past — the past, one presumes, not simply of his Serbian childhood; the past of Europe, which he retells as a succession of mini-Grimm fairy tales at their most monstrous, peopled by goblins, witches, men marching, blood and bones, phantom horses in the snow, Mongols and foxes: in short, all the paraphernalia of what he himself calls . . . The Great Dark Night of History." [2]

Simic is not a nakedly personal poet, though he does occasionally allude directly to his past. For example, "Prodigy," from *Classic Ballroom Dances* (1980), is based upon the metaphor of chess as similar to life: "I grew up bent over / a chessboard. // I loved the word *endgame*." (Even the most innocent details in a Simic poem — here the word *endgame* — seem to have sinister implications.) Later he tells us that he lived in "a small house / near a Roman graveyard. / Planes and tanks / shook its windowpanes." Of the ending of the war he says,

"I'm told but do not believe / that that summer I witnessed / men hung from telephone poles." It is not that this did not happen or that Simic was not there to see it; rather, he says, his mother "had a way of tucking my head / suddenly under her overcoat."

In prose works and in interviews, Simic has been more forthcoming on the subject of his early life than he generally is in his poems. Talking with Sherod Santos, Simic began by saying: "I had what Jan Kott calls 'a typical East European education.' He means, Hitler and Stalin taught us the basics. When I was three years old the Germans bombed Belgrade. The house across the street was hit and destroyed. There was plenty more of that, as everybody knows. When the war ended I came in and said: 'Now there won't be any more fun!' That gives you an idea what a jerk I was."[3] The mixing of seriousness and humor here is typical of Simic, a quality we see in much of his poetry; he once explained: "If I make everything at the same time a joke and a serious matter, it's because I honor the eternal conflict between life and art, the absolute and the relative, the brain and the belly, etc. . . . No philosophy is good enough to overcome a toothache . . . that sort of thing."[4]

Simic loves humor for its own sake, but it is also part of his worldview, though in an oblique sense; humor allows for a necessary sense of distancing from the harshest forms of reality, the sort of distancing he describes through an anecdote in his essay "Reading Philosophy at Night": "One day in Yugoslavia, just after the war, we made a class trip to the town War Museum. . . . Most of the space was taken up by photographs. . . . Then we saw a man having his throat cut. The killer sat on the man's chest with a knife in his hand. He seemed pleased to be photographed. The victim's eyes I don't remember. A few men stood around gawking. There were clouds in the sky."[5] The mingling of tragic event and proud indifference here is similar to the mingling of seriousness and humor in Simic's poems; he holds a dirty mirror up to the world, and what he sees reflected is deeply suffused by politics and black humor.

Which is not to say that he addresses politics directly; rather, political realities provide a constant background to the world of the poems. In fact, even when he is about his other most serious business — seeking through metaphor the veiled unities that he suspects underly the objects of the visible world —

Simic's orientation is most often political. In an essay that I will presently discuss at some length, Helen Vendler accurately assesses the value of Simic's commitment to a political vision:

> Simic . . . is certainly the best political poet, in a large sense, on the American scene; his wry emblems outclass, in their stylishness, the heavy-handedness of most social poetry, while remaining more terrifying in their human implications than explicit political documentation. In his plainness of speech, he is of the line of Whitman and Williams, but in the cunning strategies of his forms, he has brought the allegorical subversiveness of Eastern European poetry into our native practice. The next generation of political poets will be on their mettle if they want to surpass him.[6]

Simic's indirect approach to politics is nicely illustrated in "Empire of Dreams" from *Classic Ballroom Dances*:

On the first page of my dreambook
It's always evening
In an occupied country.
Hour before the curfew.
A small provincial city.
The houses all dark.
The store-fronts gutted.

I am on a street corner
Where I shouldn't be.
Alone and coatless
I have gone out to look
For a black dog who answers to my whistle.
I have a kind of halloween mask
Which I am afraid to put on.

The poem has a narrative structure, though the meaning of its story, like the meaning of its details, is more suggestive than exact. Indeed, all the poem gives us is atmosphere and setting; the absence of any real action is perhaps indicative of the speaker's (and the author's) general sense that he cannot truly control his own life. The situation that threatens him seems clearly to be political, but we are never told exactly that. Thus the poem is vaguely allegorical and resembles a parable, features that make it typical of Simic's generally allusive and indirect practice.

The world that Simic presents indirectly here is rendered more directly in one of the jottings in his notebooklike essay "Wonderful Words, Silent Truth": "I always had the clearest sense that a lot of people out there would have killed me if given an opportunity. It's a long list. Stalin, Hitler, Mao are on it, of course. And that's only our century! The Catholic Church, the Puritans, the Moslems, etc., etc. I represent what has always been joyfully exterminated."[7] What he represents is an individual, one among a great mass of people, and not a leader, not one of those who has learned to exercise power over others. While talking on television recently with Charlayne Hunter-Gault about the war between the Bosnians and the Serbs in his native land, Simic said: "I believe in individuals. My poetry speaks for all the individuals in the world." He meant, among other things, that his poems do not speak for governments.[8]

Despite its focus upon the individual, Simic's poetry seems remarkably impersonal; as one anonymous reviewer has strikingly commented, Simic does not generally write from the perspective of his own ego, but "speaks through archetypes who reside on a plane where fantasy intersects pure imagery."[9] Simic himself has said:

> I've always felt that inside each of us there is profound anonymity. . . . when you go deep inside, you meet everyone else on a sort of common ground — or you meet nobody. But whatever you meet, it is not yours though you enclose it. We are the container and this nothingness is what we enclose. . . . It is as if we were in a room from which, paradoxically, we were absent. I suppose, in some ways, this is a mystical vision that brings to me a sense of the universe as an anonymous presence.[10]

As Matthew Flamm has noticed, one aspect of this sense of anonymity is surely political, as we are "shaped by forces that couldn't care less about character. . . .

affected all of the time by things we barely understand."[11] However, Simic also uses anonymity in his quest for the mystic unity that he believes underlies the world in which we live; in his essay "Notes on Poetry and Philosophy," he relates this idea to his use of metaphor by speaking of Heidegger's "attack on subjectivism, his idea that it is not the poet who speaks through the poem but the work itself. This has always been my experience. The poet is at the mercy of his metaphors. Everything is at the mercy of the poet's metaphors — even Language, who is their Lord and master."[12]

The emphasis Simic places upon the device of metaphor seems to elevate it to another plane, that where allegory, parable, and myth reside. Indeed, Simic has defined myth specifically in terms of metaphor: "Myth: finding a hidden plot in a metaphor. There's a story and a cosmology in every great metaphor."[13] "Rough Outline," from *Austerities* (1982), illustrates this method using, as usual, a political framework for its content:

> The famous torturer takes a walk
> Whom does he see standing there in the snow
> A pretty girl in a wedding dress
> What are you doing out there all alone in the cold
>
> You're the famous torturer much feared
> I beg you to spare my love
> Who is in your darkest prison cell
> I wish to marry him etc.
>
> I will not give back your bridegroom
> He must be tortured tonight
> By me personally
> You can come along and help him lament his fate
>
> She remained where she was
> The night was cold and very long

Down by the slaughterhouse a dog-like creature howled
Then the snow started to fall again

In content, this is an utterly appalling poem; probably its worst detail is the "dog-like creature" in the penultimate line: what is it really?

But we also cannot take the poem entirely seriously, because it is so stagey and improbable. That these two characters, with so much in common, should happen to meet is serendipity by design; we suspect that the girl has been waiting there, appropriately costumed, on the chance that the torturer should pass by. And what sort of kingdom is it that has not just its famous torturer but one with so courtly a demeanor? It is of course Simic's world of dark intent, the kingdom of twentieth-century reality as portrayed in some twentieth-century poetry—the kind of poetry Simic describes in "Reading Philosophy at Night":

> Poor poetry. Like imperturbable Buster Keaton alone with the woman he loves on an ocean liner set adrift on the stormy sea. Or an even better example: Again drifting over an endless ocean, he comes across a billboard, actually a target for battleship practice. Keaton climbs it, takes out his fishing rod and bait, and fishes peacefully. That's what great poetry is. A superb serenity in the face of chaos. Wise enough to play the fool.[14]

So "Rough Outline" is also amusing, because of its incongruities, its discontinuities, its veiled uncertainties.

Simic has created a parable in the poem, an anecdote that is meant to illustrate, no matter how unrealistic it is on its surface, the true and real nature of life in much of the twentieth century. If we assume that this action is set in a country like Carolyn Forché's El Salvador, then the poem is politically true; if we assume (more fancifully) that the torturer represents the allegorical character Death and that the bridegroom has, let us say, cancer, then the poem is humanly true in a broader sense. What matters is not the creative imagination that a reader might apply to the poem, but the aura of an inescapably cruel fate that it creates. The fact that these lines are unpunctuated (except for the period after the abbreviation, which becomes amusing because of its singularity) and that the dialogue is not placed within quotation marks makes the poem even more frightening and more general; we grope through the text as through a dangerous midnight cityscape. As Simic has said: "My subject is really poetry in times of madness. . . . I am astonished, therefore, when I see that for most poetry today history does not exist. One can read literally hundreds of pages of contemporary poetry without encountering any significant aspect of our common twentieth-century existence. The poets write about Nature and they write about themselves in the most solipsistic manner, but they don't write about their executioners." [15]

In speaking of quasiallegorical or parablelike elements in Simic's poems, I mean of course to be relating those poems to the world that surrounds them and their author; I treat the poems, as I treat most poems, essentially from the perspective of mimesis. In his own discussions of these same elements, or something very similar to them, Simic seems to relate them instead to the nature of language, though his use of the word *mythic* ties what he describes to the parabolic method I have been discussing. Simic's most extended comment on this matter appears in an interview, where he says:

> It occurred to me that mythical consciousness, the kind that is still present in our world, is to be found in language. The first examples for me were idiomatic expressions using the impersonal "it" . . . [where] you have an ambiguity at the core of the expression that points to something nameless. The "it" is both minimal and all-inclusive. "It" can open up to whatever is beyond, can include all the other "its." This is a mythical situation; you eventually hear the little drama of the expression as its possibilities unfold. There's another aspect, too, as in idiomatic and figurative expressions. Take the expression, "counting bats in his belfry." Here you get [a] kind of "place" . . . ; somebody has a head that is really a belfry, and it has bats in it, and he's counting them. It's a bizarre predicament which can be dramatized by taking the line literally and ignoring the figurative intention. . . . So the mythic, then, occurs where something is transformed — the familiar is made strange, made miraculous, and it can generate a story line, a plot, a destiny. [16]

Although Simic begins this explanation by focusing on the smallest integer of any textual story, its words, he quickly moves from that minimalist level to the stories themselves, and their implications. His true interest, we must conclude, is not in the words but in the parables; not in the discrete parts but in the sense of unity that those parts might build. This is why the series of miniaturist poems on starkly individual objects that Simic wrote early in his career are much less important than was once thought. Such poems as "Fork," "Spoon," "Knife," "Ax," and "Stone," far from constituting Simic's major achievement, as some critics used to insist, actually function—and merely—as a kind of momentary stay against confusion. The general world of Simic's poems is deeply frightening, mysterious, hostile, dangerous; by focusing on such unimportant, everyday objects, he was able to achieve, however briefly, some degree of order, comprehension, and control within this world.

Indeed, Simic himself seemed to undercut the importance of these poems and this approach in "Invention of Nothing," which he placed near the end of the volume—*Dismantling the Silence*—that contains all of them:

I didn't notice
while I wrote here
that nothing remains of the world
except my table and chair.

And so I said:
(for the hell of it, to abuse patience)
Is this the tavern
without a glass, wine or waiter
where I'm the long awaited drunk?

The color of nothing is blue.
I strike it with my left hand and the hand disappears.
Why am I so quiet then
and so happy?

I climb on the table
(the chair is gone already)
I sing through the throat
of an empty beer-bottle.

Seemingly to illustrate the vacuity inherent in his devotion to such insignificant objects as the fork, spoon, knife, axe, and stone, Simic here isolates himself completely from the world, but with a set of similar objects. Lacking any frame of reference, they have no meaning; the poet is stranded in a solipsistic and nihilistic universe.

Strangely, however, he seems happy, and I think for two reasons. The first is both spurious and political: given the nature of the real world portrayed in Simic's poems, nothingness might be a sensible alternative. As Geoffrey Thurley has pointed out: "We could say that he de-creates his world in an effort to forestall its non-existence."[17] The reason this logic is spurious is that it is strictly theoretical. For Simic to destroy the world in order to forestall its destruction by the politicians and warmongers is clearly not a viable choice for him: he loves his objects far too much to want to see them destroyed. Thus his happiness on the basis of this first reason turns out to be the giddiness of the madman who has killed what he loved and now cackles on his way to hell. The second reason he is happy, the nonspurious reason, is precisely because he is in the presence of his beloved objects. Simic's attitude toward the things of this world is interesting in and of itself; it also happens to be crucial to a full understanding of his poetry. The key lies in his attitude toward metaphor, the poetic device that makes ideas out of things.

To explain Simic's attitude toward objects and the use he wishes to make of metaphor, I am going to comment at some length on Helen Vendler's recent essay on Simic's poetry, "Totemic Sifting," published in *Parnassus: Poetry in Review*. Although Vendler seems to be appreciating Simic's poetry in most of her essay, in fact she is almost entirely out of sympathy with it. Not until we read her penultimate paragraph, however, do we understand the reason. In the process of commenting on Simic's book *Dime-Store Alchemy* (1992), which contains his analysis of the art of Joseph Cornell, Vendler enunciates one of her own most deeply held beliefs about poetry:

> No other book by Simic transmits so strongly as *Dime-Store Alchemy* what New York must have meant to him when he first arrived from Europe — "A poetry slot machine offering a jackpot of incommensurable meanings activated by our imagination. Its mystic repertoire has many images."

Myself, I draw the line at words like "incommensurable" and "mystic," but that is perhaps my loss. I really do find poetry commensurable with life — not "mystic" (which for me would lessen its wonder) but rather entirely within the realm of human power, however rarely that power appears. De Chirico is quoted by Simic a few pages earlier, uttering a sentiment with which Simic explicitly agrees ("He's right"):

> Every object has two aspects: one current one, which we see nearly always and which is seen by men in general; and the other, which is spectral and metaphysical and seen only by rare individuals in moments of clairvoyance.

I could understand such a statement if it were put in terms of ascribed value. After all, a perfectly bad painting is to its maker a beloved object, as it is to some of its viewers (see, for example, Bishop's "Poem," on the bad painting by her great-uncle); and even an unlovely house is someone's castle. Perhaps the ascription of value to any object is a form of "clairvoyance," because objects look different seen with the eye of love or the eye of poetic scrutiny. But de Chirico doesn't seem to be talking about this sort of invisible halo, which we can all confer on many objects. No, some other claim is being made here. The "rare individuals" that de Chirico and Simic have in mind are artists. But is there some aspect of objects seeable only by artists? And if so, is the right word for such an aspect "spectral?" Or "metaphysical?" And if so, is a reader or viewer then privileged to see this "spectral" aspect through the eyes of the artist? Artists make us see many aspects of being, but none of them seem to me either spectral or metaphysical, nor do I feel admitted to a form of clairvoyance, in the usual occult sense of that word. I am wary of vaguely mystical claims made for poetry and the other arts, as wary as I am of ethical and civic claims, and of truth claims. There are better ways of making good citizens, or laying down laws of ethics, or providing a defense of truth-claims, than lyric poetry. Poems, like all human fabrications, from straw huts to theology, are made to our measure and by our measure, and are not above or beyond us. We do not need to ascribe more to art than we ascribe to unaided human powers elsewhere. Language and paint are not metaphysical and forms are not spectral. Patterning is a universal human act; and even when it is extended to the most complex and imaginative and individual patterning, it is still ours and of us, no more. The power of art, for me, is precisely that it does *not* belong to some rare or spectral realm. As Stevens said of the poet, "As part of nature he is part of us, / His rarities are ours." [18]

Vendler comes face-to-face here with one of the mysteries of contemporary art, and her literal (as opposed to figurative, the realm within which metaphor operates) perspective forces her to deny it its power. Earlier she had quoted Simic as saying ("in an interview almost twenty years ago"): "I don't mind admitting that I believe in God." [19] By making this statement an important cornerstone of her argument, Vendler places Simic's acceptance of de Chirico's word "metaphysical," and his own use of the word "mystic," into a religious context. But Simic has also said — and much more recently, in his gnomic series of aphorisms on poetry, "Wonderful Words, Silent Truths" — "What a mess! I believe in images as vehicles of transcendence, but I don't believe in God!" [20]

By "transcendence" I think Simic means something like an ability to overcome the limitations of ordinary perception in order to see the essential unity that he suspects exists among all things; as he also says in "Wonderful Words, Silent Truths": "Awe (as in Dickinson) is the beginning of metaphysics. The awe at the multiplicity of things and awe at their suspected unity." [21] The agency by which one might achieve this sort of transcendence, this perception of unity, is for Simic metaphor: "Metaphor offers the opportunity for my inwardness to connect itself with the world out there. All things are related, and that knowledge resides in my unconscious." [22] That is a lovely theory, but it is only a theory, and Simic knows this. He never claims success in his quest to express the essential unity of things; though he can feel the truth of his vision, he can in no way either demonstrate or prove it.

The best that he or any contemporary artist can do is continue to search for this unity, and create, through metaphor, fragmentary proofs of its existence: "Every new metaphor is a new thought, a fragment of a new myth of reality. Metaphor is a part of the not-knowing aspect of art, and yet I'm firmly convinced that it is the supreme way of searching for truth."[23] Finally, because this ideal cannot be attained, only searched for, poetry must perforce remain both fragmentary and mysterious, a matter of uncertain process rather than of certain product: "I like a poem that understates, that leaves out, breaks off, remains open-ended. A poem as a piece of the unutterable whole."[24] In an earlier essay, Simic had attempted to identify this approach as the basis for the best poetry of today: "The aim of every new poetics is to evolve its own concept of meaning, its own idea of what is authentic. In our case, it is the principle of uncertainty. Uncertainty is the description of that gap which consciousness proclaims: actuality versus contingency. A new and unofficial view of our human condition. The best poetry being written today is the utterance and record of that condition and its contradictions."[25] By "actuality" Simic means the principle of unity that underlies all reality; by "contingency" he means our flawed vision, the best that he or any contemporary poet can do.

In her essay, Vendler attempts to analyze two Simic poems in which he seems almost able to grasp, through metaphor, the ultimate truth of life in the twentieth century. The first of these—"With Eyes Veiled," from *The Book of Gods and Devils*—Vendler calls a "Black Mass parody of the religious quest":[26]

First they dream about it,
Then they go looking for it.
The cities are full of figments.
Some even carry parcels.

Trust me. It's not there.
Perhaps in the opposite direction,

On some street you took by chance
Having grown tired of the search.

A dusty storefront waits for you
Full of religious paraphernalia
Made by the blind. The store
Padlocked. Night falling.

The blue and gold Madonna in the window
Smiles with her secret knowledge.
Exotic rings on her fat fingers.
A black stain where her child used to be.

Vendler sees this poem as an explicit and seemingly literal comment on the role of religion in the modern world; that the icons are "Made by the blind," she says, "is deflationary, but worse is to come. The degradation of the Madonna into fallen woman . . . is followed by the macabre replacement of Innocence by 'a black stain.'" [27]

Though not incorrect — the meaning she sees is certainly part of the poem — Vendler's reading is too specific and limiting. The metaphors are suggestive not just of the role of religion in our world, but of the whole nature and feel of that world. As such, they should probably not be nailed down too firmly by the critic. In a comment that sounds intended for this specific poem, Simic suggests that he himself often does not know the significance of what he writes: "The poet is a tea leaf reader of his own metaphors: I see a dark stranger, a voyage, a reversal of fortune, etc. You might as well get a storefront and buy some Gypsy robes and earrings! Call yourself Madame Olga." [28]

Vendler's reading of the other of these two poems is even more obviously limiting. Of "Tragic Architecture," from *Hotel Insomnia* (1992), she says: "With the reverse prophecy of informed hindsight, Simic now knows which of his elementary school classmates grew up to go mad, to turn into a murderer, or to consent to being an executioner. The potential cruelty of all children is laconically remarked." [29] Vendler seems to assume (of her favorite poem in the book!)

that Simic is himself the speaker, that he is revisiting his childhood school, that he is commenting specifically on his actual schoolmates:

> School, prison, trees in the wind,
> I climbed your gloomy stairs,
> Stood in your farthest corners
> With my face to the wall.
>
> The murderer sat in the front row.
> A mad little Ophelia
> Wrote today's date on the blackboard.
> The executioner was my best friend.
> He already wore black.
> The janitor brought us mice to play with.
>
> In that room with its red sunsets —
> It was eternity's time to speak,
> So we listened
> As if our hearts were made of stone.
>
> All of that in ruins now.
> Cracked, peeling walls
> With every window broken.
> Not even a naked light bulb left
> For the prisoner forgotten in solitary,
> And the school boy left behind
> Watching the bare winter trees
> Lashed by the driving wind.

In fact, the poem is much larger than its ostensible setting, and again comments on the whole of twentieth-century history, not just on one classroom. It thus reaches toward parable, toward allegory, toward the power of the sort of expanded or extended metaphor that gives Simic entry into his realm of truth. As I have noted above, Vendler is very wise in discussing the political side of Simic's poetry; but the side that deals with objects and metaphors remains a mystery to her—and precisely because of the literalist doctrine she espouses in her own most heartfelt expression of her poetics. Simply put, she insists on a literal reading of these poems, and perhaps of all poems. As Simic has also said: "There are critics unable to experience the figurative, the way some people are color blind and tone deaf, or lack a sense of humor. They can tell it's a metaphor, but it doesn't do anything for them. If it cannot be paraphrased . . . it's . . . worthless." [30]

While the subject matter of most of Simic's poems is grim, their writing is not, and it is this that saves them from a hopeless and self-destructive nihilism. Even his most somber poems exhibit the liveliness of style and imagination of the sort that we have seen in "Rough Outline" and that seems to provide the possibility of joy. Perhaps a better way of expressing this would be to say that Simic shines upon the darkness of political structures the lightness of art. The unsettlingly titled "Eyes Fastened with Pins," from *Charon's Cosmology* (1977), provides an apt example of this stylistic lightness, given the focus of its attention:

> How much death works,
> No one knows what a long
> Day he puts in. The little
> Wife always alone
> Ironing death's laundry.
> The beautiful daughters
> Setting death's supper table.
> The neighbors playing
> Pinochle in the backyard
> Or just sitting on the steps
> Drinking beer. Death,
> Meanwhile, in a strange

Part of town looking for
Someone with a bad cough,
But the address somehow wrong,
Even death can't figure it out
Among all the locked doors . . .
And the rain beginning to fall.
Long windy night ahead.
Death with not even a newspaper
To cover his head, not even
A dime to call the one pining away,
Undressing slowly, sleepily,
And stretching naked
On death's side of the bed.

Simic's poems achieve both their meanings and their aesthetic effects through manipulation of image and statement; the sound devices that we attend to in the work of other poets have little bearing in his. He works more in an intellectual mode than in an aesthetic mode and is more interested in working out intriguing mind games than in creating sensual delights.

Most of the irony in this poem is transparent: rather than an invincible force with awesome powers, Death is presented as an ordinary working guy, something like a traveling salesman who cannot find his clients. His family is nuclear, and his neighbors are regular guys, pinochle players with, perhaps, names like Chuck Charon, Harry Hephacstus, Pete Prometheus, and Hermes Hanson. A more ambiguous irony enters the poem near the end, however, when Death cannot find a dime for the telephone. Who does he want to call? The most obvious possibility is his wife — except that she is presented earlier not as panting with passionate loneliness but as ironing Death's shirts. No, the person waiting for Death's call is the one he is on his way to visit, the person whose turn it is to die. The poem thus seeks to unite Thanatos not with any old mortal, but with Eros. This turnabout is surprising but appropriate within the skewed universe of Simic's poems.

Since the appearance of his *Selected Poems*, Simic has published five new books of poems, four of them significant volumes that indicate in their varied ways his publishing history. The first of these four, *Unending Blues* (1986), is unique for being the only one among Simic's many books that seems mostly coherent thematically. Surely, however, Robert Atwan overstates the case when he says of this volume that "It reminds us that a new book of poems can be a literary item in itself and not just a miniature anthology of a poet's latest efforts. So intertwined are all of the 44 poems in this book that each poem seems to reflect all of the others, an aesthetic accomplishment that becomes apparent only after several re-readings. The impression is of poems without clear verbal boundaries, poems that drift unendingly in and out of each other."[31] In a moment I will give my own sense of this book's casual coherence; for now I will point out that most other critics seem to agree with me that, in general, Simic writes books that are more like "miniature antholog[ies]" than like carefully designed wholes. In reviewing *Selected Poems*, for example, Michael Milburn said that "in seeking patterns and developments over the course of the seven books excerpted here, one concludes that each poem's quality has little to do with when it was written or the company it keeps." Similarly, Matthew Flamm suggests that Simic "tends to write too many of the same kind of poem. . . . You have to pick and choose with Simic."[32]

I think it is this very lack of attention to thematic coherence that has given Simic a spotty reputation, the kind of reputation that would allow the Pulitzer Prize committee to overlook his selected volume. A reader has to take care to distinguish the best poems in a Simic collection; otherwise one could be distracted by the lesser poems into thinking that Simic is just fooling around. Such is the conclusion that Edward Larrissy came to in reviewing *Austerities*: "The fact that Simic has a taste for compressed ironic narratives means that the overall impression is of a series of grim or black-humorous anecdotes. Sometimes the anecdotes, or the irony attached to them, can seem slight." More significantly, David Dooley found himself able, even in reviewing *Selected Poems*, to dismiss Simic as a copycat jokester: "Simic has been content to drift with the tide. Over the years he has been influenced by most of the quasi-surreal trends that came along. He has written deep image poems. . . . He has written the three kinds of poems Robert Peters . . . described as 'catatonic surrealism': instruction or recipe poems . . . , poems which resemble fairy tales . . . , and paranoid quasi-narratives. . . . Simic's best [!] work has affinities with Gary Larson's *Far Side* cartoons." [33]

Ironically, the weakest of Simic's books is the one that finally won him the Pulitzer Prize, *The World Doesn't End* (1989). The volume consists primarily of quips and anecdotes, most of them written in prose, that rarely get above the level illustrated by "History Lesson," which reads, in its entirety: "The roaches look like / Comic rustics / In serious dramas." More interesting is *The Book of Gods and Devils*, which mostly treats Simic's early days living in New York City. Perhaps Simic's best volume, however, is his most recent, *Hotel Insomnia*, some poems from which I shall analyze at the end of this essay. First, however, I would like to take a brief look at *Unending Blues*, toward the end of which subtle forces of change seem briefly to undermine Simic's Kafkaesque vision. The stance taken in the earlier poems of this book, however, is the one with which we are already familiar. "Dark Farmhouses," for example, deconstructs the sense of order we expect to underlie an everyday scene seemingly taken from the real world:

Windy evening,
Chinablue snow,
The old people are shivering
In their kitchens.

Truck without lights
Idling on the highway,
Is it a driver you require?
Wait a bit.

There's coal to load up,
A widow's sack of coal.

Is it a shovel you need?
Idle on,
A shovel will come by and by
Over the darkening plain.

A shovel,
And a spade.

A threatening world is created in the first stanza and deepened thereafter; something like the state is conspiring against widows and other old folks, taking away their coal and preparing to bury them anonymously. The imagery is suggestive but imprecise, familiar but hauntingly unreal. The shovel and spade seem like dark knights in some chivalric romance; they bring death, seemingly at the behest of a truck that has been personified into the technological overseer of eternal destruction.

In its austerity of both image and narrative, the poem is representative of most of Simic's work. Almost as though to acknowledge this characteristic himself, Simic begins another poem in this book: "I only have a measly ant / To think with today. / Others have pictures of saints, / Others have clouds in the sky." As *Unending Blues* progresses, however, we begin to see a change away from this sense of Kafkaesque terror. Again there are lines that seem to explain what is going on: "He was writing the History of Optimism / In Time of Madness." Characterizing the twentieth century as a time of madness is entirely in character for Simic; writing a history of optimism is not. And yet that is precisely what he ends up doing in this volume, in an understated way and with some backsliding. The geographical pattern the book falls into is one indication of this; section one is set in the Europeanized city of dark intent so familiar in all of Simic's work. The poems of section three, however, are set almost entirely in the country, in a place relatively sequestered from the faceless and soulless technological forces of the modern world. The first sign of this change in setting appears in a twisted bucolic image — in "Department of Public Monuments" — that the reader cannot help but see, on first reading, as ironic: "If Justice and Liberty / Can be raised to pedestals, / Why not History? // It could be that fat woman / In faded overalls / Outside a house trailer / On a muddy road to some place called Pittsfield or Babylon."

That Simic (or his speaker) actually might care for this woman becomes a possibility when she makes a second affectionate appearance in another poem, called "Outside a Dirtroad Trailer," that begins: "O exegetes, somber hermeneuts, / Ingenious untanglers of ambiguities, / A bald little man was washing / The dainty feet of a very fat woman." The pattern of fat-woman love reaches its climax in the volume's concluding poem, "Without a Sough of Wind":

Against the backdrop
Of a twilight world
In which one has done so little
For one's soul

She hangs a skirt
On the doorknob
She puts a foot on the chair
To take off a black stocking

And it's good to have eyes
Just then for the familiar
Large swinging breasts
And the cleft of her ass

Before the recital
Of that long day's
Woes and forebodings
In the warm evening

With the drone of insects
On the window screen
And the lit dial of a radio
Providing what light there is

Its sound turned much too low
To make out the words
Of what could be
A silly old love song.

Silly old love song indeed. It seems impossible not to conclude that Simic has arranged the poems in this book so that they will end up contradicting his title. Though blues they may often be, these certainly are not blues unending. A tone of affection enters, lightly sounded, midway through the book; it later grows in power and range until it drowns out most wailing by the end. It is the presence of love in this book that most counters the threat of political murder and existential disorder that permeates Simic's vision of the world. In another of his notebook jottings, this one defining his practice in terms of Nietzsche, Simic seems to explain the impulse toward love in his work: "Nietzsche: 'A small overstrained animal whose days are numbered' proposes the 'object of its love.' That's what my poems are about." [34]

That happiness is not Simic's true poetic metier, however, seems conclusively proven by an unusually undistinguished group of nine poems placed at the beginning of the third section of *Hotel Insomnia*. Perhaps the weakest of these is the happiest, a poem called "Spring" that, given its setting and expression of love, might have appeared at the end of *Unending Blues*:

This is what I saw — old snow on the ground,
Three blackbirds preening themselves,
And my neighbor stepping out in her nightdress
To hang her husband's shirts on the line.

The morning wind made them hard to pin.
It swept the dress so high above her knees,
She had to stop what she was doing
And have a good laugh, while covering herself.

The opening stanza is promising; it establishes a scene and setting in which many things could happen. But instead of having a torturer step out from behind a shrub, or sending a vulture to peck out the woman's eyes, Simic merely reports on the cozy action of an ordinary gust of wind.

Elsewhere in this volume we find some of Simic's best poems, including four prose pieces that might have been designed to overcome the lingering negative impression created by the prose poems in *The World Doesn't End.* "The Inanimate Object," for example, begins:

> In my long late night talks with the jailers, I raised again the question of the object: Does it remain indifferent whether it is perceived or not? (I had in mind the one concealed and found posthumously while the newly vacated cell was fumigated and swept.)
>
> "Like a carved-wood demon of some nightmarish species," said one. "In cipher writ," said another. We were drinking a homemade brew that made our heads spin. "When a neck button falls on the floor and hardly makes a sound," said the third with a smile, but I said nothing.

Perhaps the first thing we notice in these stanzas is the indifference of these characters to the plight of the dead prisoner; rather than talk about him, they choose instead to debate their version of one of the oldest philosophical questions in existence, the one that asks: If a tree falls in the middle of a forest with no one close enough to hear, does its falling make a sound? The speaker of the poem is restrained; while withholding his real subject (and, we suspect, his feelings) from his companions, he tries to maintain a neutral attitude in the debate. The jailers, meanwhile, are sardonic and witty, and seem mostly concerned with their own quippy repartee. In truth, they are commenting not on the question ostensibly raised by the speaker but on the question he is keeping to himself, the one concerning the dead prisoner. The answers they give are distinctly unsettling: the first jailer seems to describe himself and his colleagues as nightmarish demons; the second seems to describe the way they are talking now, in riddles; the third seems to describe something of a process whereby the late prisoner lost his life as his neck button spun to the ground.

In the concluding two paragraphs of the poem, the speaker turns back to himself, his thoughts, the kind of life he is living:

> "If only one could leave behind a little something to make others stop and think," I thought to myself.
>
> In the meantime, there was my piece of broken bottle to worry about. It was green and had a deadly cutting edge. I no longer remembered its hiding place, unless I had only dreamed of it, or this was another cell, another prison in an infinite series of prisons and long night talks with my jailers.

The dead prisoner obviously did leave behind something that made others stop and think, and the conclusions we have reached are far from comforting, either to us or to the speaker of the poem. The object hidden by the speaker suggests similar conclusions — the jagged glass is sharp enough to kill *him* — while the ending of the poem suggests that the lessons of this series of events are broadly applicable, having something to do with human life generally, perhaps. Because he chooses to write in myths and parables, Simic invites us to make such extensions.

At the beginning of this essay I discussed "A Letter," in which Simic declined the invitation he issued to himself to remember, nostalgically, an old love affair. In another of the prose poems in *Hotel Insomnia* he accepts this invitation; the result is "Miss Nostradamus":

> Once I adored a seeress, a long-legged one. We roamed the streets of New York like dreamy newlyweds trailing a funeral of some lofty vision.
>
> "It's like glimpsing the world's secret among the empty aquariums and bird cages in the back of a dime store," she told me between kisses.
>
> And then late one night, with eyes veiled as the sirens sounded:
>
> "Overcoats thrown over their pyjamas, the lovers of tragedies now stand

in ecstacy, there where a naked babe is being thrown out of a high window by a woman in flames."

Life in the modern city—and not just New York, but any city—for Simic invites insights like these: all lofty thoughts and visions are dead and being buried; such meaning as remains may be found at the backs of dime stores; now our most ecstatic moments come only through instances of tragic and meaningless death.

"Street Scene," perhaps the ultimate poem in Simic's corpus, occurs near the end of *Hotel Insomnia*. Rather than New York it is set in an anonymous city, a generalized city, an allegorical city, the city occupied by all citizens of Simic's twentieth century. There we see:

A blind little boy
With a paper sign
Pinned to his chest.
Too small to be out
Begging alone,
But there he was.

This strange century
With its slaughter of the innocent,
Its flight to the moon —
And now he waiting for me
In a strange city,
On a street where I lost my way.

Hearing me approach,
He took a rubber toy
Out of his mouth
As if to say something,
But then he didn't.

It was a head, a doll's head,
Badly chewed,
Held high for me to see.
The two of them grinning at me.

The message of this blind seer, the illegitimate son of Miss Nostradamus perhaps, is delivered not in words but through an image. Here near the end of
"This strange century," near the end of Simic's most recent book, this word-
less and sightless beggar of a boy, himself an innocent victim, becomes both
prophet and executioner, becomes prophet as executioner, becomes prophet
of random, meaningless, borderless, thoughtless execution; execution of casual
pleasure, momentary pleasure, the instinctive, barely noticed pleasure of the
drooling boy.

In his autobiographical essay, Simic tells another story that seems oddly appropriate to the atmosphere and meaning of this poem. He was walking the
streets of Belgrade with a friend during the war when they "met a pack of children . . . who said that they were from the circus":

> It was true. There used to be a circus tent on the fairgrounds in the early
> years of the war, but now only a few trailers were left on its edge. These
> were odd-looking children. They wore the strangest clothes — unmatched,
> wrong-sized costumes — and they jabbered, speaking a foreign language
> among themselves.
>
> "Show him what you can do," said my friend, who had met them before.
> They obliged. A little boy stood on his hands. Then, he removed one hand,
> and was left for a moment standing on the other. A thin, dark-eyed, dark-
> haired girl leaned back until her head emerged from between her legs.
>
> "They have no bones," my friend whispered. The dead have no bones, I
> thought. They fall over like sacks of flour.[35]

I think this story can be interpreted in two quite different ways, both of them
appropriate to Simic's poems. From one perspective, we might say that the circus children in this anecdote, like the blind boy in "Street Scene," seem all but
dead themselves: they are refugees in the war-torn city, foreigners with no

homes and scarcely enough clothing to keep them warm. Their lives have no meaning beyond their chatter and tricks; there is no such thing as a future. Without the stability, the sense of certainty, provided by those metaphoric bones, the movements of their bodies are as unpredictable as everything else in their lives.

However, those movements are also energetic and free, even joyful. The circus children do not seem at all depressed; their situation may—or may not—be tragic from the point of view of the two observers, but it is definitely not tragic from their perspective. Just as they seem to enjoy the freedom inherent in having bodies without "bones," they seem also unconcerned by the other deprivations and limitations of their lives. Although everything that has happened to them has happened without their volition or control, they are enjoying, or at least making the most of, their situation. Interestingly, in an important passage near the end of the autobiographical essay, Simic places himself as poet in an almost identical situation: "My father used to ask me jokingly, 'Where are we going to immigrate next?' Anything was possible in this century. The experiment was still in progress. People like him and me were its laboratory animals. Strangest of all, one of the rats was writing poetry." [36]

Although among the poets studied in this book Ashbery is the one with the best theoretical understanding of the principle of uncertainty, Simic is the one with the deepest instinctive understanding of its workings within the real world, the everyday world, the social and political world of the second half of the twentieth century. Thus he uses in the passage I have just quoted the language of laboratory science—in this case that of biology—to describe the position occupied by anyone who happens to have lived on this planet since the advent of the Second World War. It might be objected that Simic is talking not about everyone, but only about those people who were displaced from their homes by the war. To maintain such a position, however, a reader would have to ignore nearly all of the poems so far discussed in this essay; clearly Simic believes that we are all displaced persons, no matter the outward circumstances of our lives.

Were we to translate the terms he uses into the language of physics, we might say that Simic sees himself, his father, and all the rest of us as electrons, quarks, subatomic particles; as unpredictable entities emphatically not in charge of their own destinies; as creatures of which an experimenter could say with certainty only this much: "When we see one of these fellows streaking pell-mell through the void, we can have only a probabilistic notion of where it is headed and of what might happen next; of course something completely surprising could happen instead. If we look at two of these creatures, we become correspondingly less certain of the future of either. Were we to look at 250 million of them at once, meaning roughly the entire population of the United States, we would have no idea whatsoever of where any single one of them might go next, though the general tendency of the crowd would be quite obvious."

By now it ought to be clear how and where the crowd in Simic's twentieth century is collectively moving — randomly, uncertainly, and arbitrarily toward sudden, certain, and unforeseen annihilation; this general tendency is easy enough to see. Individual cases, however, are not so predictable, and that is why the average poet, the average reader, the average middle-class citizen of the United States may still envision living, even in 1997, the dream of Robert Browning's character Pippa, who was thoroughly convinced that "God's in his heaven, all's right with the world," the dream of living in an orderly, predictable, deterministic, Newtonian universe. Simic certainly does not express such a perspective in his poems; he does not even hint at it, except through laughter. Ashbery hints at it all the time, but always from a position of befuddlement, vague longing, and irony; the individual life may well turn out to fit such a pattern, but only by accident, and unpredictably.

At least in his more recent poems, Dobyns writes from a different, and sadder, perspective. Most of his characters long for order; perhaps because most of them lived when they were younger in orderly worlds that made some kind of sense, they seem to think that such orderliness is the norm against which the tangled lives they are living today can be measured. Because of their expectations, these characters seem generally disappointed at the way things have turned out; though they may joke and make fun, in fact they are chronically depressed. Although Dobyns lives and writes from within the same world of uncertainty that Simic occupies, he understands it differently. Thus the characters in his poems seem mostly to fight against that world. The exception to this pattern is found in poems such as those in *The Balthus Poems*, where the poet, rather than dealing more or less feebly with forces beyond his control, asserts his own ability to create a world of art in which anything can happen if he wants it to.

I believe it is the clarity of Simic's vision that gives rise to his sense of pleasure, his joy, his humor; because his expectations are so low, so attuned to the unreliable operations of reality, he seems able to appreciate the occasional happy accident. Thus Simic occupies a position different from those of both Dobyns and Ashbery. Dobyns seems trapped within a world of uncertainty that he does not fully understand; though he sometimes seizes the opportunity it offers to assume the role of creator, more often he allows himself to be defeated by it. Ashbery, on the other hand, seems to have an instinctive, surprisingly profound — and almost certainly unconscious — theoretical understanding of the principle of uncertainty; he uses it both as the basis of his form, the how of his writing, and as the basis of his content, the what of his writing.

The situation for Simic is quite different: fully aware of uncertainty, unpredictability, randomness, he turns these things to his advantage. The odd sense of joy we find expressed in even his darkest poems shows his inherent acceptance of the principle of uncertainty as the nature of being. We might say that he writes his poems from the perspective of a subatomic particle: though he knows he has been somewhere, he has no idea why; though he knows where he is now, he does not know if he will still be there one second from now, and again he does not know why. As for the future, he does not know if there is one, and certainly he does not know why there may or may not be one. Finally, he does not know even his own makeup, the nature of his own being, whether he is ultimately composed of matter, or of energy, or of both. What makes Simic so unusual a poet is his acceptance of a state of existence so defined; in his eyes it seems to be not mere being, but *being*, the way existence is, the whole eternal neverending unpredictable indeterminate uncertain and undying dynamic ongoing process of the universe of which we are, unaccountably, a part.

Of the poets whose work is studied in this book, only two — Ashbery and Simic — seem demonstrably aware of living in a world of uncertainty, to the point of being able both to express and to accept such a situation. Though the other poets may be said to live and write from within a world of uncertainty, none of them shows the level of awareness that would be necessary for them to address this situation philosophically—whether explicitly or implicitly—as I have argued that both Ashbery and Simic do. Instead, we will see Gerald Stern, Stanley Kunitz, and Charles Wright reacting to a world they do not fully understand, in much the general way we have already seen Dobyns reacting to it. Each of them knows that the old ways of understanding have died; each of them searches for some new way to understand reality, some new basis from which to react to it. Thus we will see them assessing the world in which they live and searching for something to cling to, something in which to believe.

Gerald
Stern

Weeping and Wailing and Singing for Joy

Though born in 1925, Gerald Stern did not publish his first book until the age of forty-six, in 1971. Not many readers noticed either that volume, *Pineys*, or *Rejoicings: Poems, 1966–1972* (1973), and probably for an excellent reason: the poems in them are neither particularly impressive nor (a closely related point) much like Stern's later, most characteristic work. "There among the Delectables" is typical:

I have fallen to pieces
over Romanticism.
I have fought at the back door,
dreaming of taking you *a la sinistra*;
it was my secret dream,
there among the delectables,
each with the same vice.
You are huge as an elephant.
The mistake was in assuming
you existed at all.

Although written in a first-person voice, like Stern's mature poems, this piece is different in almost all other respects. Where later poems are expansive both in line and overall length, this one is short, with clipped lines. It also seems unusually concerned to make its point, not that that point is especially clear: is the poem about sexual desire? literary preference? the delusion of thinking someone exists? all of the above?

One reason we cannot tell is that the poem is niggardly in its supply of details; it seems to want to deal with the world through relatively abstract statements rather than through concrete images. The typical later Stern poem is profusely detailed and imagistic; it accumulates events, objects, memories, opinions, desires, regrets (the list could go on almost endlessly) while hiding the more abstract point (if there is one) that gives these things continuity.[1] Finally, the voice that speaks "There among the Delectables" is not intimate; it does not even hint at the miracle that most characterizes the use of voice in later poems, the way Stern's consciousness saturates that of the reader, the way he draws us into the poem, makes us participate in its actions, empathize with its feelings, agree with its opinions. Judging by the fact that he did not reprint the poem in *Leaving Another Kingdom: Selected Poems* (1990), it would appear that Stern himself more or less concurs with my judgment of "There among the Delectables."

Stern entered his real career with *Lucky Life*, published as the Lamont Poetry Prize selection in 1977. Like all the later collections, this one has no discernable thematic structure; in each book the poems accumulate in a more or less random fashion for approximately eighty pages, and then they stop. Almost as though to prove that he had no deep purpose in ordering the poems in his individual volumes, Stern made two significant alterations in organizing *Leaving Another Kingdom*. First, he deleted an unusual number of poems from each unit: *Rejoicings* had forty-five poems as a separate book and has only sixteen in the selected; *Lucky Life* had fifty-one poems and there has thirty-five; *The Red Coal* (1981) had forty-nine and there has thirty-seven; *Paradise Poems* (1984) had fifty-six and there has thirty-seven; and *Lovesick* (1987) had forty-six and there has thirty-four. The second clear indication of structural looseness is that

Stern chose to lead off each of the sections of his selected volume with a poem that appeared much later in its separate volume. The prominence thus accorded these poems seems intentionally placed, for each expresses an important concern of Stern's work generally. I will discuss several of these key poems later in this essay.

Rather than any progression of theme, what holds Stern's poems together, both individually and as a group, is the personality of their speaker. As Frederick Garber has pointed out, Stern "and the world are evenly matched" in the poems; "[i]ts business is to be what it is, his to be the self which mourns and rejoices but also the self that makes this world happen over again in words."[2] Stern's voice is as concerned with self-definition as Walt Whitman's; by far the favorite pronoun of both poets is *I*. Indeed it is in the way each of these poets uses a highly personalized speaking voice that Garber finds the greatest connection between them: "If [Stern] has been called our Whitman, that comes from the expansiveness, the ebullience, the openness of voice in these poems; the occasional catalogues matter less than the large exuberance of the voice."[3] Nearly every one of Stern's poems begins by locating his speaker in terms of space, time, mood, and topic of immediate interest. Using a process something like free association, Stern then will accumulate memories, objects, scenes, and events, all of them relevant to the matter at hand. The poems are filled with segues, leaps, changes in subject and direction. And, again like Whitman's poems, they are basically happy, though darkness does certainly appear.

In his most powerful and typical poems, Whitman overcomes tragedy and feelings of depression not only through his transcendentalist philosophy but also through his manipulation of style and voice — particularly, with regard to the former, his use of language, rhythm, and imagery, and, with regard to the latter, his widely varied modulations of tone, including a buoyancy that denies all depression: "I do not snivel that snivel the world over, / That months are vacuums, and the ground but wallow and filth; / That life is a suck and a sell, and nothing remains at the end but threadbare crape, and tears."

More often than not, Whitman's subject matter is dark, tragic; the role that voice, attitude, and belief play in overcoming these things is obvious. Less obvious to too many readers are elements of form, especially those of surface form. An outstanding example is provided by his "Reconciliation":

> Word over all, beautiful as the sky,
> Beautiful that war and all its deeds of carnage must in time be utterly lost,
> That the hands of the sisters Death and Night, incessantly softly wash
>   again, and ever again, this soil'd world;
> For my enemy is dead, a man divine as myself is dead,
> I look where he lies white-faced and still, in the coffin — I draw near,
> Bend down and touch lightly with my lips the white face in the coffin.

Almost always in his best poetry Whitman relies on a combination of iambic and anapestic measures to reinforce his powerful sense of buoyancy. The richest and most effective line in this poem, the third, illustrates the method beautifully: it begins with a pair of relatively relaxed anapests, moves through a series of evermore insistent iambs, and concludes with the powerfully spondaic effect of "this *soil'd world.*" Hypnotically beautiful by itself, this rhythm is supported, as always in Whitman, by a generous use of both assonance and consonance (this particular line is dominated by a consonantal pattern based on the letters *d* and *s*). Such traditional rhetorical devices as parallelism and balance — both of them frequently signaled by repetition — are also important to the effects achieved by Whitman. To see these things at work in this poem the reader needs only to identify such repeated words and phrases as "beautiful," "that," "is dead," "white fac'd," and "in the coffin." All of these devices appear prominently in the work of Stern as well, marking another area of resemblance between the two poets.

The most significant way in which Stern differs from Whitman is philosophical; Stern is able to discover no theoretical, metaphysical layer of belief underlying his accumulation of basically raw data, nothing akin to the transcendentalism that suffuses Whitman's poems. However often Stern utters the plea we hear in the poem "I Need Help from the Philosophers," from *Lucky Life*—"Oh I need help from Spinoza. / I don't want to grab Dante by the finger and ask him about my lost woods. / I don't want to hang around like Proust in the damp privies"—the fact is that he never gets any real help from the philosophers. Though he certainly does not hang out in privies, Stern nearly always operates on the level of concrete reality and seeks his answers there. Lacking an Oversoul, with no sure way to transcend death, he is an earthbound Whitman, limited to telling us how it is with him, what the world looks and sounds like, how it tastes, feels, and smells.

"Immensity," from *The Red Coal*, Stern's fourth collection overall and the second in his mature phase, uses metaphor to give the poet's fullest and most direct explanation of where he searches for materials and meanings and what helps him there:

> Nothing is too small for my sarcasm. I know
> a tiny moth that crawls over the rug
> like an English spy sneaking through the Blue Forest,
> and I know a Frenchman that hangs on the closet door
> singing *chanson* after *chanson* with his smashed thighs.
> I will examine my life through curled threads
> and short straws and little drops of food.
> I will crawl around with my tongue out, growing
> more and more used to the dirty webs hanging
> between the ridges of my radiator and the huge
> smudges in that distant sky up there, beginning
> more and more to take on the shape of some great design.
>   This is the way to achieve immensity, and this is the
> only way to get ready for death, no matter what Immanuel Kant
> and the English philosophers say about the mind,
> no matter what the gnostics say, crawling
> through their vile blue, sneezing madly in the midst of that
> life of theirs, weighed down by madness and sorrow.

Like "There among the Delectables," this poem is also somewhat atypical of Stern's general practice because it has so clear an abstract point and because it proves it so relentlessly. However, that point is fully in line with the spirit and the practice of Stern's later work, as is the heavy use of concrete imagery.

Stern makes his first metaphorical leap in line four, where the second insect is referred to directly as a Frenchman, without the intervening level established with the moth — described as being *like* an Englishman. Stern begins his major metaphorical strategy in line six, where the speaker himself becomes these (and presumably other) insects. Thus Stern's way of understanding "immensity" (meaning something like the significance of everything) is not through studying the philosophers, so amusingly depicted at the end of the poem, but through taking the closest, most minute look possible at the details of reality.

I have said that Stern is an essentially happy, lighthearted poet. In "Making the Light Come," from *Lovesick*, his sixth collection, he himself points out that he has had actually two different ways of being happy, one in his earlier work and one in his mature poems. "My pen was always brown or blue, with stripes / of gold or silver at the shaft for streaks / of thought and feeling," he says, but always then, in the early days, "I turned my face to the light." Remembering how James Wright, in his very last poems, turned his own face to the light, basking with the lizards he loved, we might wonder how anything could be better. But Stern claims to have found another way:

> I was worshipping
> light three dozen years ago, it led me
> astray, I never saw it was a flower
> and darkness was the seed; I never potted
> the dirt and poured the nutriments, I never
> waited week after week for the smallest gleam.
> I sit in the sun forgiving myself; I know
> exactly when to dig. What other poet
> is on his knees in the frozen clay with a spade
> and a silver fork, fighting the old maples,
> scattering handfuls of gypsum and moss, still worshipping?

The contemporary American painter John Winship, one of whose paintings adorns the cover of this book, has explained the prevalence of darkness in his work. He always begins a painting by laying a dark background on the canvas, then builds by adding elements of light—a procedure the opposite of what most painters do. When asked why, Winship replied that in his view this method conforms better to the essentially dark and uncertain nature of reality.

Many poets (and physicists) would agree that light is the exception in our universe, which began as nothing but a black, blank immensity and is still suffused by that. Stern seems to accuse himself of being superficial by ignoring the presence of darkness in his early poems. Whether that is true or not, he does not ignore it in his later work, though he characteristically always arrives at the light. Again his method may not be all that different from that of Whitman, who says at the end of "Song of Myself," his masterpiece: "I bequeathe myself to the dirt, to grow from the grass I love; / If you want me again, look for me under your bootsoles."

"Blue Skies, White Breasts, Green Trees," from *Lucky Life*, is a typical Stern performance and one of his best mature works. It begins with the speaker again castigating himself for not seeing the real nature of the world:

What I took to be a man in a white beard
turned out to be a woman in a silk babushka
weeping in the front seat of her car;
and what I took to be a seven-branched candelabrum
with the wax dripping over the edges
turned out to be a horse's skull
with its teeth sticking out of the sockets.
It was my brain fooling me,
sending me false images,
turning crows into leaves
and corpses into bottles,
and it was my brain that betrayed me completely,
sending me entirely uncoded material,
for what I thought was a soggy newspaper

turned out to be the first Book of Concealment, written in English,
and what I thought was a grasshopper on the windshield
turned out to be the Faithful Shepherd chewing blood,
and what I thought was, finally, the real hand of God
turned out to be only a guy wire and a
pair of broken sunglasses.
I used to believe the brain did its work
through faithful charges and I lived in sweet surroundings for the brain.
I thought it needed blue skies, white breasts, green trees,
to excite and absorb it,
and I wandered through the golf courses dreaming of pleasure
and struggled through the pool dreaming of happiness.

The propensity to seek out brightness, and to manufacture it when it is not there, is well established by these lines, which themselves are more subtle than their message. We note Stern's heavy reliance on the rhetorical device of parallelism, a technique that James Wright discussed and praised at length (along with balance, antithesis, and periodicity) in the talk that he delivered at the English Institute in 1962, "The Delicacy of Walt Whitman."[4]

The first two objects that are compared through parallelism in this poem (the man in a white beard and the woman in a silk babushka) are presented quite straightforwardly, in both meaning and phrase; the second two (candelabrum and horse's skull) are far more complicated. Generally speaking, the further Stern goes with a parallel series, the more intricate become its integers, the more resonant its meanings. Even the second of the first two images above is more complex than the first, thanks to the additional material presented in the third line — "weeping in the front seat of her car" — to which nothing in the first image compares. These additional elements are present, however — and in an increasingly complicated fashion — in ensuing images. And while the comparison of the candelabrum to the horse's skull is much denser than anything earlier, it is not as dense as the three pairs of what-I-thought-was-this-turned-out-to-be-that images that follow. The middle one of those (the apparent grasshopper that is actually the Faithful Shepherd) is especially tangled because of the way it seems to reverse both the pattern and the meaning of the series. It would be wrong to conclude that Stern nods in such cases; rather, he is complicating the question of how his speaker perceives and misperceives reality by injecting an appropriate layer of uncertainty and ambiguity.

Similar reversals take place in the second half of the poem, which begins with the speaker enunciating how his vision has changed:

Now if I close my eyes I can see the uncontrolled waves
closing and opening of their own accord
and I can see the pins sticking out in unbelievable places,
and I can see the two lobes floating like two old barrels on the Hudson.
I am ready to reverse everything now
for the sake of the brain.
I am ready to take the woman with the white scarf
in my arms and stop her moaning,
and I am ready to light the horse's teeth,
and I am ready to stroke the dry leaves.
For it was kisses, and only kisses,
and not a stone knife in the neck that ruined me,
and it was my right arm, full of power and judgment,
and not my left arm twisted backwards to express vagrancy,
and it was the separation that *I* made,
and not the rain on the window
or the pubic hairs sticking out of my mouth,
and it was not really New York falling into the sea,
and it was not Nietzsche choking on an ice cream cone,
and it was not the president lying dead again on the floor,
and it was not the sand covering me up to my chin,
and it was not my thick arms ripping apart an old floor,
and it was not my charm, breaking up an entire room.
It was my delicacy, my stupid delicacy,
and my sorrow.
It was my ghost, my old exhausted ghost,

that I dressed in white, and sent across the river,
weeping and weeping and weeping
inside his torn sheet.

Powerful waves of parallelism carry the reader insistently through these
lines, both straightforwardly and in their careful modulations. When Stern announces his readiness to reverse everything, we expect that he is going to begin
seeing ugliness where beauty exists. What he ultimately means is that he will
expand his scope, by attending also to the sorrow of the world, to the extent of
celebrating and comforting it. His reversal is still more profound than this,
however, for by the end of the poem he is blaming not his cold lack of vision
for his errors, but his newfound compassion — his delicacy, his sorrow, his
torn-shirt weeping.

This reversal is no more accidental than the reversals seen earlier: Stern does
not wish to go from one extreme to another; thus he will not become a vast be-
wailer in his poems but will continue to praise and celebrate. Now, however, he
will celebrate in full recognition of the dark soil from which all light must grow.
As he puts it in another poem: "I am singing / in harmony, I am weeping and
wailing." Jane Somerville — Stern's most serious critic — points out that he
needed the fall, the weeping, to attain the fullest level of joy, the singing, in his
work: "In Stern's plot, we are lucky to have lost paradise. It is a nostalgic entity
which exists because it is lost. We are lucky to suffer, since suffering is what we
transcend. Acknowledgment and acceptance of suffering is our humanity, our
victory. This is a version of the romantic vision, and it is also the tragic vision,
in which spiritual redemption is won through noble suffering." [5]

Perhaps it is this sense of a lost paradise that accounts for the presence of
so much nostalgia in Stern's poetry — though I have also heard him condemn
(while speaking to my class in contemporary American poetry at Gettysburg
College) "the mere self-indulgence of nostalgia." [6] What he prefers to nostalgia
is the resurrection possible through the agency of memory, whereby paradise
seems to come back to life. As David Wojahn has said, "everything Stern sees is
filtered through the process of memory, and . . . is given clarity and integra-

tion. . . . Memory, for Stern, becomes the great equalizer. It allows everything in the poet's experience to co-exist. He wants his walks in Paris in 1950, his reading of Zane Grey novels as a child, and his drives through contemporary Pittsburgh to seem all to happen at once."[7] In "Leaving Another Kingdom," the title poem of his selected volume, Stern's speaker is visited at his house on the Delaware River in Pennsylvania by fellow poet Philip Levine. Talking about the old days, the two writers walk through a landscape rich with the glories of nature, roses and mud and stones and robins. Reaching the river they wade out to an island where the talk and the watching continue. Eventually they walk again "into the water, / leaving another island, leaving another / retreat, leaving another kingdom." Both nature and the past are made paradisal and timeless in this poem.

The love of nature, its glorification, its importance to his version of the human enterprise, is everywhere in Stern's poems, though perhaps nowhere more clearly than in "Cow Worship," with which he chose to begin the *Red Coal* section of the selected poems:

I love the cows best when they are a few feet away
from my dining-room window and my pine floor,
when they reach in to kiss me with their wet
mouths and their white noses.
I love them when they walk over the garbage cans
and across the cellar doors,
over the sidewalk and through the metal chairs
and the birdseed.
—Let me reach out through the thin curtains
and feel the warm air of May.
It is the temperature of the whole galaxy,
all the bright clouds and clusters,
beasts and heroes,
glittering singers and isolated thinkers
at pasture.

He loves nature best, that is, when it is most recognized as an intimate part of the human environment — or should we say when the inevitable human participation in the world of nature is most clear. Thus he loves the cows best when they invade the farmhouse, loves the "clouds and clusters" when they can be seen as "beasts and heroes," loves the clouds and galaxies best when they are recognized as part of the human, "glittering singers and isolated thinkers / at pasture."

Another poem that celebrates both nature and the past, from Stern's recent book *Bread without Sugar* (1992), is "One Day an Arbor Vitae," about his childhood quests and rituals in Pittsburgh. Stern grew up in an orthodox Jewish family, and it is to that experience and its concern with dietary laws and ways of worship that he ascribes his lifelong obsession with rituals; in his everyday life, Stern told my students at Gettysburg College, "I go through different kinds of ritual behavior, as I like to do in my poems." "One Day an Arbor Vitae" begins by describing his youthful explorations:

I always went for natural shapes, I slid
on the mud to get away from my street, I ripped
my leather jacket on the hill hanging on
to a broken branch; I swung there, one foot turned,
one foot almost lost. It took me an hour
to find a certain willow; I say an hour
but it was more like twenty minutes. I went
to the roundhouse and back in fifteen or twenty minutes,
I went to the station itself in half an hour.
Six in the morning was my time, I picked up
three kinds of grass, I wrapped them in my notebook.

This search for a natural paradise is not a pastoral search, for it takes place within an urban environment. Thus, in addition to the roundhouse and the station, the seeker also encounters a wrecked and abandoned truck, a tire, other rubbish, and a predatory city cat that wants to catch the crows who are feasting on a dead opossum. Eventually:

          I broke a stick
before I climbed the hill, it helped me think,
one day it was a sword, one day a crutch,
one day it was a broom. I held it up
with two of my fingers, I smashed some branches, I cut
some ugly roots, it helped me sleep at night,
having it there beside my bed, leaving it
behind the door, either inside or outside.
One day it was an insect, one day a flutist
leaning with one arm out and one leg splattered;
one day an arbor vitae, one day a maple.

If the setting itself and its variety of objects seems not exactly paradisal, certainly the memorial Stern has constructed to them is; the poem, like so many of these poems, creates its own paradise out of unlikely parts. Ultimately what is most celebrated in Stern's work is the imagination, as used long ago by the boy, as featured now in the work of the mature poet.

A more complex paradise is created in "The Dancing," which Stern uses to lead off the *Paradise Poems* section of the selected poems. The poem is an ecstatic tour de force, written in a single sentence celebrating the end of the Second World War:

In all these rotten shops, in all this broken furniture
and wrinkled ties and baseball trophies and coffee pots
I have never seen a post-war Philco
with the automatic eye
nor heard Ravel's "Bolero" the way I did
in 1945 in that tiny living room
on Beechwood Boulevard, nor danced as I did
then, my knives all flashing, my hair all streaming,
my mother red with laughter, my father cupping
his left hand under his armpit, doing the dance
of old Ukraine, the sound of his skin half drum,

half fart, the world at last a meadow,
the three of us whirling and singing, the three of us
screaming and falling, as if we were dying,
as if we could never stop — in 1945 —
in Pittsburgh, beautiful filthy Pittsburgh, home
of the evil Mellons, 5,000 miles away
from the other dancing — in Poland and Germany —
of God of mercy, oh wild God.

All of the familiar Stern rhetorical devices are present here, in this poem of implicit and ironic joy, a strange and bitter sense of reconciliation, at the end not just of the war but of the Holocaust.

Darkness takes many forms in Stern's poems — we read tender elegies for his father and sister, laments over the unfortunate life and death of his friend Bob Summers, poems of homage to the lonely and poor — but what seems to concern him most deeply and most often is the persecution of the Jews, and the most resonant poem on this topic is "Soap," from *Paradise Poems*. The underlying subject matter here is nothing short of horrible, though horror is not the primary effect established by the opening stanza:

Here is a green Jew
with thin black lips.
I stole him from the men's room
of the Amelia Earhart and wrapped him in toilet paper.
Up the street in *Parfumes*
are Austrian Jews and Hungarian,
without memories really,
holding their noses in the midst of that
paradise of theirs.
There is a woman outside
who hesitates because it is almost Christmas.
"I think I'll go in and buy a Jew," she says.
"I mean some soap, some nice new lilac or lily

to soothe me over the hard parts,
some Zest, some Fleur de Loo, some Wild Gardenia."

What we first notice of course is the amusing surface texture of the lines — that
and their insistence that all soap, particularly post–World War II concentration
camp soap, is made from the bodies of Jews.[8] Lying behind the poem is our
knowledge that the Nazis actually perpetrated this horror; Stern uses that fact
in a wildly hyperbolic fashion in order to make his point — that the persecution of Jews is not an occasional matter.[9]

However, it is the charm of this writing that is most significant, because of
its trenchant beauty, because of the astonishing discordancy that it raises. The
effectiveness of Stern's discursive (as opposed to his more strictly rhetorical)
poems depends heavily upon the atmosphere they create at length — depends,
that is, more upon matters of deep form than matters of surface form. Isolated
lines and sentences tend to sound more like whimsical prose than like rich,
Whitmanian singing. Stern's rhythms develop through long passages and depend as much upon the manipulation of subject and imagery as upon the
modulation of syllables.[10] In the second stanza of "Soap," the speaker is inside
the shop that sells soap:

And here is a blue Jew.
It is his color, you know,
and he feels better buried in it, imprisoned
in all that sky, the land of death and plenty.
If he is an old one he dances,
or he sits stiffly,
listening to the meek words and admiring the vile actions
of first the Goths and then the Ostrogoths.
Inside is a lovely young girl,
a Dane, who gave good comfort
and sad support to soap of all kinds and sorts
during the war and during the occupation.
She touches my hand with unguents and salves.

She puts one under my nose all wrapped in tissue,
and squeezes his cheeks.

Though these lines do gain some unity from Stern's customary sort of repetition—the parallelism inherent in "listening to the meek words and admiring the vile actions" and the outright repetition in Goths and Ostrogoths—primarily they concentrate on subject matter and on the outrageousness of the extended soap metaphor. The Danish girl seems clearly to belong to the time of the Holocaust, the most prominent frame of reference for this poem. The inclusion of the fourth- and fifth-century invaders of the Holy Roman Empire extends Stern's web and further generalizes his point.

The action becomes more domestic, more intimate, in the third and fourth stanzas; the third concentrates upon a single Jewish character, a single piece of soap:

I buy a black Rumanian for my shelf.
I use him for hair and beard,
and even for teeth when things get bitter and sad.
He had one dream, this piece of soap,
if I'm getting it right,
he wanted to live in Wien
and sit behind a hedge on Sunday afternoon
listening to music and eating a tender schnitzel.
That was delirium. Other than that he'd dream
of America sometimes, but he was a kind of cynic,
and kind of lazy—conservative—even in his dream,
and for this he would pay, he paid for his lack of dream.
The Germans killed him because he didn't dream
enough, because he had no vision.

The "logic" of this story is that the Jew was exterminated by the Germans because he did not act on his dream and emigrate to America (emigrating to Vienna would not have done much good)—as though he could have emigrated anywhere. Of course the logic is Teutonic, and Stern's irony is bitter and palpable. The stanza also illustrates another general trait of Stern's poetry; like Whitman, he has the ability to inhabit other characters, to become them, to know their minds, bodies, and actions. Thus do both writers expand the intimacy and scope of their poems.

Domesticity continues in the fourth stanza, which returns us to the base location of the poem while again extending its range of characters and time:

> I buy a brush for my back, a simple plastic
> handle with gentle bristles. I buy some dust
> to sweeten my body. I buy a yellow cream
> for my hairy face. From time to time I meet
> a piece of soap on Broadway, a sliver really,
> without much on him, sometimes I meet two friends
> stuck together the way those slivers get
> and bow a little, I bow to hide my horror,
> my grief, sometimes the soap is so thin
> the light goes through it, these are the thin old men
> and thin old women the light goes through, these are
> the Jews who were born in 1865
> or 1870, for them I cringe, for them
> I whimper a little, they are the ones who remember
> the eighteenth century, they are the ones who listened
> to heavenly voices, they were lied to and cheated.

The emphasis early in this stanza upon the speaker's toilette makes us focus on his body and therefore on bodies generally, on those that were gassed seeking cleanliness in the "showers" at Auschwitz. The link is through flesh, its fragility, its mutability. Later in the stanza Stern uses the setting in which he speaks the poem to include elderly Jews who are living in America. At the end of this poem we will learn that it was written at Christmastime in 1982; in making the people he meets on the street 112 or 117 years old, Stern is again using hyperbole. He does it in order to extend his range once more, but this time what he expands is the scope of his blame: the implicit promises of God, made in more certain times, were not kept.

In his long, final stanza Stern further personalizes the poem by concentrating upon a single piece of soap, a single other character, whom eventually he addresses, but not at first:

> My counterpart was born in 1925
> in a city in Poland — I don't like to see him born
> in a little village fifty miles from Kiev
> and have to fight so wildly just for access
> to books, I don't want to see him struggle
> half his life to see a painting or just to
> sit in one of the plush chairs listening to music.
> He was dragged away in 1940
> and turned to some use in 1941,
> although he may have fought a little, piled
> some bricks up or poured some dirty gasoline
> over a German truck. His color was rose
> and he floated for me for days and days; I love
> the way he smelled the air, I love how he looked,
> how his eyes lighted up, how his cheeks were almost pink
> when he was happy. I loved how he dreamed, how he almost
> disappeared when he was in thought. For him
> I write this poem, for my little brother, if I
> should call him that — maybe he is the ghost
> that lives in the place I have forgotten, that dear one
> that died instead of me — oh ghost, forgive me! —
> Maybe he stayed so I could leave, the *older* one
> who stayed so I could leave — oh live forever!
> forever! — Maybe he is a Being from the other
> world, his left arm agate, his left eye crystal,
> and he has come back again for the twentieth time,
> this time to Poland, to Warsaw or Bialystok,

to see what hell is like. I think it's that,
he has come back to live in our hell, if he could
even prick his agate arm or even weep
with those crystal eyes — oh weep with your crystal eyes,
dear helpless Being, dear helpless Being. I'm writing this
in Iowa and Pennsylvania and New York City,
in time for Christmas, 1982,
the odor of Irish Spring, the stench of Ivory.

We do not realize it for the first eleven and one-half lines here, but of course this is another character conjured from a bar of soap. Again Stern creates a whole life for the character, inhabits him, absorbs his being into the poem.

First we see him in his own element: his impoverished life in Poland, his "useful" extermination. Then, after establishing the source of this character in a bar of rose soap, Stern personifies him, recreates him once more, from the odor that clings to his own body after he bathes. As he apostrophizes this character, the speaker attempts to figure out the relationship that exists between them. First the Jew is seen as a younger brother, probably because of his diminutive size as a piece of soap. Then he romantically becomes the older brother, the one who stayed behind so our speaker could escape the Nazis. Finally—when the pressure of reality becomes too much for the speaker to bear—the Jew becomes an angel, someone who does not suffer, who comes to earth and endures extermination as a kind of experiment.

And the painfulness of this subject matter *is* too much to bear; though many other possibilities present themselves on a moment's reflection, the Holocaust probably remains the closest thing to an unspeakable horror in human history. So Stern's speaker must eventually escape from an ultimate facing of its reality; the psychological pressure, the empathy he feels, is simply too great. The movement here is the opposite of what we see in another of the lead-off poems in *Leaving Another Kingdom*, "Behaving Like a Jew," which opens the *Lucky Life* section; Stern's speaker discovers a dead opossum on the road and decides that he is sick of all this death and needs to pay attention to it: "I am going to be unappeased at the opossum's death. / I am going to behave like a Jew." It is the depth of Stern's empathy, balanced by his resilient buoyancy, that allows for the wonderful texture of "Soap," which is playful, amusing, tragic, intriguing, absorbing. Earlier, I commented on how Whitman could create beauty from ugliness by presenting tragic events and details in his customary style. Here — and in many other poems — we see Stern doing the same thing. It is among the many shared traits that bind them.

As we learn from the extreme attention he pays to soap and other objects in the poem, and in the other poems we have looked at, Stern is an exemplary realist, a lover of the things of this world. So pervasive is this fascination that the reader does occasionally think that this is all there is in his poetry; a love of objects and the narratives that hold them together. We have also seen several thematic concerns that belie this superficial impression; ultimately, however, the element that most gives unity and substance to Stern's poems is not theme but personality: things are always tied to people in his poems, and both of these are always filtered through the consciousness that pervades every line. I have also said that the most common pronoun in this poet's body of work — as it is in Whitman's — is the first-person, personal *I*; the central placement of the self in Stern's poems is clearly indicated in "The Bite," chosen by Stern to begin not only the *Rejoicings* section of his selected poems but the entire selected poems, since the *Rejoicings* section is first. The commitment to an autobiographical agenda is unmistakable:

I didn't start taking myself seriously as a poet
until the white began to appear in my cheek.
All before was amusement and affection —
now, like a hare, like a hare, like a hare,
I watch the turtle lift one horrible leg
over the last remaining stile and head
for home, practically roaring with virtue.
    Everything, suddenly everything is up there in the mind,
all the beauty of the race gone
and my life merely an allegory.

When asked by my students to say something about the progress of his writing career, Stern replied that he started to write when he was eighteen or nineteen years old and published some poems in good magazines. Then he spent almost twenty years burning his writings; his most productive hours were devoted to being a teacher, husband, and father. By the time he was thirty-eight he thought he had wasted his chance to be a writer, so badly out of touch was he with the literary age. It was only after a period of depression and the giving up of all sense of ambition, he says, that he began to write his real poems. "The Bite" is spoken from the perspective of the despair that Stern felt when he realized his age and lack of achievement.

Ultimately, what Stern really celebrates in his poems is not just the self and not just brute reality; his deepest commitment is to these two things as they are brought together by his consciousness and his imagination. Like the quantum physicists who formulated the Copenhagen interpretation, Stern recognizes that the observer of reality is also a creator of reality. It is his own awareness of things that most concerns him, his ability to praise them, to see connections among them, to realize their beauty and significance. Stern's love for things is therefore profound; he wallows in them and gazes at them, long and long. And from this act of contemplation, this interaction between the dumb object and the mind of man, comes light. Without the world of substances, understanding is so much gas; without consciousness, the world is just dumb things. Consciousness is soul for Stern; it is the perceiving, describing, connecting, *insighting*, enlivening mind of the poet that gives meaning and structure to existence.[11]

Such a vision lends importance, profundity, even a sort of sanctity, to the simplest and most common objects. For example, "A Song for the Romeos" — which is dedicated to "my brothers Jim Wright and Dick Hugo" — is about, as a footnote explains, "a kind of indoor/outdoor slipper or sandal":

I'm singing a song for the romeos
I wore for ten years on my front stoop in the North Side,
and for the fat belly I carried

and the magic ticket sticking out of my greasy hatband
or my vest pocket,
the green velvet one with the checkered borders
and the great stretched back with the tan ribs
going west and east like fishes of the deep looking for their covers.

I'm wearing my romeos
with the papery thin leather
and the elastic side bands.
They are made for sitting,
or a little walking into the kitchen and out,
a little tea in the hands,
a little Old Forester or a little Schenley in the tea.

I'm singing a song for the corner store
and the empty shelves;
for the two blocks of flattened buildings
and broken glass;
for the streetcar that still rounds the bend
with sparks flying through the air.

And the woman with a shopping bag,
and the girl with a book
walking home one behind the other,
their steps half dragging, half ringing,
the romeos keeping time,
tapping and knocking and clapping on the wooden steps
and the cement sidewalk.

The poem is an elegy and a remembrance for Wright and Hugo, both of whom
had died by the time it was written. Its approach to the poets is oblique, the
point of connection coming through the everyday objects and way of life cele-

brated by this poem as well as most of their poems. And the title embodies a pun; all three of these writers love the common things of American life: they are indeed "the romeos." As is almost always true in Stern's work, the poem gains most of its music and verbal continuity from his use of balance, repetition, and parallelism.[12]

Stern loves the old things and the old ways — of the old country and the immigrants, but even more so those of the real America, which he celebrates every chance he gets, in "A Song for the Romeos" as in "Home from Greece" (in *Lucky Life* but not reprinted in *Leaving Another Kingdom*):

You can have the Old Causeway Inn on a Saturday night
with two hundred people waiting to get at the fish platters;
I will walk down the road to Stewart's
and sit at the counter with my watery root beer.
And you can have the future home of the Frenchtown Roller Rink
if I can have the field with cows grazing on silk and alfalfa;
and you can take Memory Town, U. S. A.,
and Land of Make Believe and Story Book Forest
if you give me an old bathtub on legs,
if you give me Nate's Pub buried in Spotswood.

We must not let Stern's desire to be alone fool us; he is celebrating the rejected fish platters as much as the watery root beer. Or as he says in "The Days of Nietzsche" (also from *Lucky Life* but also not reprinted): "when I stop to think / I know I am where I should be — I let the old restaurants / fill my soul — I let my feelings take over."

Despite his recognition of darkness, his sorrow at the Holocaust, his hatred of the Nazis, his strong sense of aging, debilitation, and loss, Stern is still primarily a poet of the light, a poet of praise, even a poet of ecstasy. Most of his poems express this outlook, but perhaps none does it better than "Grapefruit," from *Lovesick*. As usual, the poem begins by locating the speaker and establishing his mood:

I'm eating breakfast even if it means standing
in front of the sink and tearing at the grapefruit,
even if I'm leaning over to keep the juices
away from my chest and stomach and even if a spider
is hanging from my ear and a wild flea
is crawling down my leg.

Which leg? we impulsively want to ask — but it is no good wondering whether
all the details are true in Stern's poems; if they feel right to him, if they seem de-
manded by the flow of the narrative or the rhetoric of the argument, then in
they go. After these lines, the speaker looks through his wavy and dirty kitchen
window at the "useless rhubarb," the "lettuce and spinach too old for picking,"
the "thin tomato plant," and thinks of "the saints" eating thistles while standing. He imagines holding "a puny / pinched tomato in my open hand," holding
"it to my lips. Blessed art Thou, / King of Tomatoes, King of grapefruit."

After a few lines grousing about the foods he was forced to eat as a child, the
speaker begins to enter a state of ecstasy, still standing and eating grapefruit:

I bend
my head forward, my chin is in the air,
I hold my right hand off to the side, the pinkie
is waving; . . .
oh loneliness, I stand at the sink, my garden
is dry and blooming, I love my lettuce, I love
my cornflowers, the sun is doing it all,
the sun and a little dirt and a little water.

At this point there is an invisible pause for time to pass; now it is afternoon and
the poet is outside:

I lie on the ground out there, there is one yard
between the house and the tree; I am more calm there
looking back at this window, looking up

a little at the sky, a blue passageway
with smears of white — and grey — a bird crossing
from berm to berm, from ditch to ditch, another one,
a wild highway, a wild skyway, a flock
of little ones to make me feel gay, they fly
down the thruway, I move my eyes back and forth
to see them appear and disappear, I stretch
my neck, a kind of exercise. Ah sky,
my breakfast is over, my lunch is over, the wind
has stopped, it is the hour of deepest thought.
Now I brood, I grimace, how quickly the day goes,
how full it is of sunshine, and wind, how many
smells there are, how gorgeous is the distant
sound of dogs, and engines — Blessed art Thou,
Lord of the falling leaf, Lord of the rhubarb,
Lord of the roving cat, Lord of the cloud.
Blessed art Thou oh grapefruit King of the universe,
Blessed art Thou my sink, oh Blessed art Thou
Thou milkweed Queen of the sky, burster of seeds,
Who bringeth forth juice from the earth.

The poem turns into an ecstatic prayer of praise for the spirit that animates nature. Ultimately this is the most typical attitude we encounter from Stern's
expansive, praiseful, and Whitmanian speaker, an attitude that is carried as
much by the style of these poems, their repeated and modulated rhetorical patterns, as by their content, the sentiments that they express. Indeed, the only
element typical of Stern's work generally that is not present in "Grapefruit" is
his deep awareness of the tragedy that also underlies human life. But we get that
aplenty elsewhere, as I have shown, the "weeping and wailing"; in this poem we
must be content to hear Stern "singing / in harmony."

Despite the buoyancy of his vision, his sense of the holiness of things, Stern
still obviously feels himself surrounded by a world awash in cruelty and unpredictably. His poems are vastly different from those of Ashbery, though not be-

cause of any fundamental difference in the ways they view the twentieth-century world. But their rhythms are different, the ways they present their imagery and organize their ideas, the ways in which they place their lines on the page. The most important difference between them, however, occurs in the area of personality, in the voices that they choose to speak their poems. Whereas Stern's speaker does things like sweat, fornicate, garden, and noisily eat grapefruit and fish platters, Ashbery's speaker seems to float — a commentator more than a participant — on an elegant, airy cloud of frightened semi-comprehension.

With Simic, Stern shares most obviously an interest in the actions of the Fascists and the Nazis during the Second World War, though the rhythms of their poems — Stern expansive and Simic minimalist — could hardly be more different. We have seen Dobyns, too, express some interest in totalitarian politics, though the cruelties of the world of his poems are more likely to be metaphysical, interpersonal, and psychological than are those of Stern and Simic. Meanwhile, Ashbery's view of the world's waywardness is also more abstract than concrete, more similar to Dobyns' view than to that of either Simic or Stern.

Despite the various differences among them, these four poets do share — quite importantly — one fundamental response in their poems: each relies heavily on humor to mitigate, however slightly, the horror and unpredictability that they perceive in the world, the philosophical and physical uncertainty. It is in this area that we will find Charles Wright, the final poet I will discuss in this book, most different from Ashbery, Dobyns, Simic, or Stern. Humor does play a role in his poems, but only a small one. Perhaps this is because Charles Wright's general vision of things is more otherworldly than theirs; he is alone among this group in seeming to take seriously the notion of a spiritual world, a world of things unseen. Rather than use humor to forestall fear, then, Wright relies on his own peculiar brand of mysticism, of which we will see a great deal more in a moment.

Charles
Wright

Resurrecting the Baroque

Loosely speaking, the baroque impulse in contemporary American poetry is recognizable for the same reason the baroque has always been recognizable: its use of a style tending toward ornateness, even overdecoration. In art and architecture this style is characterized by ornamentation and curved rather than straight lines; in music it is characterized by embellished melodies and fugal or contrapuntal forms. In poetry it is characterized by lushness of both sound — the sort of stylistic complications chiefly of rhythm, internal harmony, and sentence structure favored by writers as diverse as Gerard Manly Hopkins and the early John Berryman — and image — an extravagant use of metaphor.

The baroque style is not a recent phenomenon; it was prominent among the British metaphysical poets of the early seventeenth century and has also been used in this country, both by such late-seventeenth-century writers as Edward Taylor and Anne Bradstreet and (albeit in a much watered-down form) by such early-twentieth-century writers as John Crowe Ransom and Richard Wilbur. In his standard work on the subject, *The Baroque Poem: A Comparative Study*, Harold Segel explains that baroque poets of the seventeenth century tended to favor the metaphor over other poetic devices:

The metaphor allowed the poet a richer, more provocative use of his imagination, his *inventiveness*, and the metaphor, because it establishes *identity* rather than merely likeness, is bolder, more difficult, and potentially more successful poetically in view of its greater capacity to excite wonderment. Certainly no other feature of Baroque poetry stands out as sharply as the extensive use of metaphor; and it was this feature, above all others, that incurred the disfavor of later ages.[1]

What contemporary baroque poets primarily have in common with their ancestors is their extensive reliance upon the device of metaphor—though certainly they do not all use metaphor in the same way. It is in the area of subject matter that we will find the most difference between the early baroque poets and the contemporary baroque poets. In the seventeenth century, the baroque was a religious art form that used symbolism to express mystical concepts: "The usually clear, sharp division in mannerism between the spheres of earth and spirit faded before the Baroque vision of the indivisibility of man's world and God's."[2] Most contemporary poets who use the baroque style use it to secular ends; such is the case with Stanley Kunitz, though he does flirt at times with prehistoric, urmythic materials. Because of the vaguely spiritual questions raised in his work, however, Charles Wright is somewhat closer to the practice of the seventeenth-century writers.

In the contemporary baroque poem, then, we might expect to find these characteristics: ornamentation or a sensual richness of imagery; metaphor or a doubling of imagery; a rich and varied use of verbal effects; a tendency toward obscurity and fragmentation; a self-conscious interest on the writer's part in his art; suggestions of the mystical within the physical; intellectuality. The work of Wright embodies these characteristics to a considerable degree. Not only will we find a good bit of progression within the body of his work, but we will also find him reaching for the unseen world in subtle ways. Wright began his career with an interest in the possibilities of form—language, image, metaphor, cadence—and has become the contemporary American poet who most exemplifies the metaphysical dimension of the earlier versions of baroque poetry.

Kunitz is more exclusively concerned with the physical and concrete; his commitment is to emotion, passion, the promptings of the human heart. He uses metaphor in both a primary sense, to relate thing to thing, and hyperbolically, to emphasize or even to exaggerate the expression of his feelings. Kunitz is perhaps best known, however, for the revolution in his style that occurred with the poems of *The Testing Tree*, published in 1971, twelve years after he was awarded the Pulitzer Prize for his *Selected Poems*. Robert Lowell (echoing virtually all the criticism devoted to Kunitz since that time) praised the volume for reflecting what he called "the drift of the age," a movement away from tortured formality and toward prosaic relaxation, away from metaphor and indirection and toward clarity, the literal truth.[3] Kunitz himself explained the change in this way: "A high style wants to be fed exclusively on high sentiments. Given the kind of person I am, I came to see the need for a middle style — for a low style, even, though that may be outside my range."[4] The statement assumes that the voice of a poem ought in some way to reflect the personality of the poet: the style is the man.

I think we have a clear enough notion of the kind of man Stanley Kunitz is. Some of his poetry is politically based, and his stance is consistently democratic in the best sense of the word; he sides with the people against the tyrants, as his longterm commitment to the poets of the Soviet Union proves. He would seem to have, in short, greater emotional affinity with the middle or low than with the high. But it is a curious fact that the most flat and least satisfying — even least characteristic — pieces in *The Testing Tree* are the political poems and the translations (which are themselves almost exclusively political, coming from such writers as Akhmatova, Mandelstam, and Yevtushenko). Among the rest of the more recent works, the weakest are consistently those that most adamantly display the low or middle style, poems such as "Words for the Unknown Makers," "My Sisters," and "Journal for My Daughter."

Kunitz is at his best today and has always been at his best when writing in an elevated, rhetorical style. Daniel Halpern tells the story of how Kunitz' devotion to style first manifested itself: "Stanley's own literary recognition came early. It began in the fourth grade, when his teacher read aloud his essay entitled 'The Father of Our Country.' It began like this: 'George Washington was a tall, petite, handsome man.' Stanley says of this seemingly contradictory offering, 'Of course I had no idea what "petite" meant, but I loved the sound of it. . . .' This love of sound, the sound of words, has never ceased — it has become the personal mark he has stamped on contemporary poetry."[5]

Perhaps the problem with Kunitz' justification of his change in method lies in its first sentence, where the poet describes what he is rejecting: "A high style wants to be fed exclusively on high sentiments." We will soon be looking at the high style but for now we might ask — what are high sentiments? Kunitz makes his early work sound like a series of lofty moral maxims, suitable for high-toned greeting cards or Victorian tea parties. In truth, the elevation visible in his strongest poems comes not from their high sentiments but from the powerful range of emotions that they enunciate.[6] I would amend Kunitz' statement to read thusly: *Powerful emotions in poetry are best presented through a powerful and rhetorical style.* Whatever his social and political commitments, Kunitz is not a man of tepid emotions, and his more tranquil and reflective poems, which appear most frequently in his later work, suffer because of their too-easy truths and their stylistic blandness.

Among the many exceptions to this pattern in Kunitz' later work is the complex and unified "The Knot," first published in *The Poems of Stanley Kunitz, 1928–1978* (1979):

I've tried to seal it in,
that cross-grained knot
on the opposite wall,
scored in the lintel of my door,
but it keeps bleeding through
into the world we share.
Mornings when I wake,
curled in my web,
I hear it come
with a rush of resin
out of the trauma
of its lopping-off.

Obstinate bud,
sticky with life,
mad for the rain again,
it racks itself with shoots
that crackle overhead,
dividing as they grow.
Let be! Let be!
I shake my wings
and fly into its boughs.

This powerful lyric is dramatic in tone and takes its strength from the skillful manipulation of several poetic devices. Perhaps the first thing that strikes the reader is the insistence of the rhythm; though the lines are loosely iambic and vary from three beats to two beats in length, they make powerful use of jammed stresses to indicate the speaker's intensity. The stress pattern is made still more prominent through heavy use of assonance, consonance, and internal rhyme. Moreover, the individual sentences open with strong, dramatic phrases and end abruptly, always at the conclusion of a line.

In the way it handles meaning the poem is not literal, not direct, not in any way plain; it is, rather, firmly grounded in the suggestive obliquity of metaphor. The message, to which the poet has a strong emotional commitment, concerns growth, rebirth, freedom, a release back into life from dormancy. The painted-over knot is (against reality) allowed this process, in part through the agency of the speaker's dream. As for the speaker himself, his role is represented metaphorically, in terms of a sleeping caterpillar ("curled in my web") that emerges to "shake my wings / and fly." The story the poem tells is archetypal, even mythic, and is similar to that told in many of Kunitz' best poems. He has described the pattern himself: "my impulse towards form generally tends to move along the lines of certain ineluctable archetypes, particularly those of death and rebirth, the quest, and the night-journey (or descent into the underworld). In all three patterns — which may be consubstantial — the progress is from a kind of darkness into a kind of light."[7] This pattern (the three paths are indeed consubstantial in Kunitz' poems) is especially prominent in the earlier work. When it is absent from the later work, the poems suffer from a lack of both thematic and artistic intensity; when it is present, as in "The Knot," we suddenly see the true consistency in this man's art and life.

Kunitz' poems are delivered in a bold, dramatic, authoritative voice that heightens and generalizes every issue. We could almost think that we were listening to an Old Testament prophet or chronicler.[8] Some of this effect is owing to the portentous narrative form in which the poems are cast; we are led to feel that they tell stories of awesome importance. This quality is apparent in the opening lines of many poems, as we are plunged into a powerful story of timeless relevance. For example, each of these passages is the opening of a different poem and each is cast almost in the form of a parable:

Time swings her burning hands
I saw him going down
Into those mythic lands
Bearing his selfhood's gold . . . .

* * *

Soul of my soul, in the ancestral wood
Where all the trees were loosened of their leaves
I strayed . . . .

* * *

Within the city of the burning cloud,
Dragging my life behind me in a sack,
Naked I prowl . . . .

* * *

Concentrical, the universe and I
Rotated on God's crystal axletree . . . .

Each of these openings announces a location for the action that is to follow, and it is never an ordinary place. We seem transported instead to the mythic realm of the ancient gods, a place where shaggy trees tower over drifting and enshrouding mists while deep and threatening noises echo from afar. In language, rhythm, and imagery these lines also seem to promise events and meanings of enormous consequence.

Which gives rise to an interesting contradiction inherent in Kunitz' early poems: often their subject matter turns out to be less significant than the style in which it is delivered. This is a hallmark of one type of the baroque contemporary poem. As an example I offer Kunitz' typical early piece, "No Word" (1944), which presents ghosts, beasts, and a smoky uratmosphere in which the speaker seems to be suffering the tortures of some extreme emotional sundering:

> Through portal and through peristyle
> Her phantom glides, whose secret mouth,
> The absence of whose flagrant smile,
> Hangs on my chimney like a wreath of cloud.
>
> I prod the coals; my tortured faith
> Kneels in the blaze on melting paws;
> Jeweled with tears, the lonely beast
> Bequeaths me irony and claws.
>
> No message. May the mothering dark,
> Whose benediction calms the sea,
> Abater of the atrocious spark
> Of love and love's anxiety,
>
> Be kind; and may my self condone,
> As surely as my judge reprieves,
> This heart strung on the telephone,
> Folded in death, whom no voice revives.

Again the poem begins by specifying a location; we seem to be in a temple haunted by the ghost of a woman. The speaker's faith in her becomes through the agency of metaphor a beast that prays in the fire, disregarding its "melting paws." The long, final sentence delivers its own double prayer—that the "mothering dark" be "kind" and that the speaker's self may "condone . . . this heart."

Why? What is the problem occasioning all this splendid, baroque rhetoric? The answer to that question hinges both on the middle phrase of the poem, "No message," and on one of its concluding images: "This heart strung on the telephone." We gradually come to realize that the problem here is that the speaker's girlfriend (apparently now his former girlfriend) is not calling him on the telephone; he is receiving "No Word." Kunitz translates this mundane situation into an impressive sequence of metaphors strung together by powerful rhythms, regular rhymes, and hints of the otherworld. We might also note in passing the heavy reliance here on adjectives—"secret mouth," "flagrant smile," "tortured faith," "melting paws," "lonely beast," "mothering dark," "atrocious spark"—a technique that would ruin a more plain poem.

Kunitz learned his trade largely from the seventeenth-century British metaphysical poets—Donne and Herbert to be sure, but also their more baroque followers, Crashaw, Vaughn, Carew.[9] Most of these are religious poets, though their vision—explicitly Christian—seems to postdate Kunitz' interest in the primitive beginnings of things by a good many years, or eons. "Among the Gods," another of Kunitz' early poems (it was first published in the *Selected Poems* of 1958), is an ars poetica that indicates the mythic context of his work while illustrating his use of baroque metaphors:

Within the grated dungeon of the eye
The old gods, shaggy with gray lichen, sit
Like fragments of the antique masonry
Of heaven, a patient thunder in their stare.

Huge blocks of language, all my quarried love,
They justify, and not in random poems,
But shapes of things interior to Time,
Hewn out of chaos when the Pure was plain.

Sister, my bride, who were both cloud and bird
When Zeus came down in a shower of sexual gold,
Listen! we make a world! I hear the sound
Of Matter pouring through eternal forms.

In another poem from the same period, Kunitz describes his heart as being
"less Roman than baroque," and surely we see little classical restraint in the
imagery of these lines.

The most persistent image in the poem is that of the stone in its many
guises, both metaphorical and real. In the first stanza, it forms both the walls of
the "dungeon of the eye" and the "antique masonry / Of heaven" at the same
time as it becomes the substance out of which the "old gods" are made. In the
second stanza, it forms the speaker's "Huge blocks of language," which emerge
"out of chaos." In the final stanza, it becomes molten, a different sort of building material for the poet's rich constructions. Throughout he allies himself
with that which is most substantial and ancient in the worlds both of myth and
of matter, grounding his work on the oldest, firmest, and most elemental of
foundations.

Elsewhere Kunitz' materials can be far more supple, though his images are
no less extravagant. The following lines from "The Way Down" are reminiscent
of the more organically oriented work of Kunitz' friend Theodore Roethke:

Air thickens to dirt.
Great hairy seeds that soar aloft
Like comets trailing tender spume
Break in the night with soft
Explosions into bloom.
Where the fleshed root stirs . . . .

It is interesting that this poem does not regularly rhyme, no more than does
"Among the Gods." Showing again his willingness to do anything that will ad-
vance the poem, however, Kunitz does break briefly into rhyme. The images
here are as hyperbolic as those in the other passages I have quoted, a quality

that surely results from the great energy of feeling that Kunitz injects into everything he writes. His love of rhetoric, metaphor, parable, and lushness of imagery and sound is forever pushing him to the extreme edge of the possibilities of language.

Such excess is of the essence of Stanley Kunitz and shows his singularity. He has never been short on self-knowledge and has always had the wisdom to keep faith with himself, his voice.[10] For example, when two of the participants in a symposium on his poem "Father and Son" objected to one of its images — in which the boyish speaker walks forth, "The silence unrolling before me as I came, / The night nailed like an orange to my brow"—Kunitz defended himself at some length, concluding: "Such moments in a poem, evident only by the pressure building behind them, can never fully explain themselves, but the poet must take his risk with them, as an article of faith. In the end, for whatever it may be worth, they constitute his signature."[11] The speaker has been stunned by his visionary meeting with his dead father; Kunitz expresses this strong emotion through an equally strong metaphor, and that gesture ultimately defines the baroque signature with which Kunitz signs his poems.

Charles Wright is the author of eight separate, "major" volumes (all but one of them published by large, well-known publishers) in addition to several "minor" volumes (small press chapbooks). Wright has divided the major volumes into two groups of four by gathering them, respectively, into a selected and a collected volume. The first four books — *The Grave of the Right Hand* (1970), *Hard Freight* (1973), *Bloodlines* (1975), and *China Trace* (1977)—appear together, some of them partially, in *Country Music: Selected Early Poems* (1982), while the later four books — *The Southern Cross* (1981), *The Other Side of the River* (1984), *Zone Journals* (1988), and *Xionia* (1990)—appear together, all of them entirely, in *The World of the Ten Thousand Things* (1990). The attentiveness to form — specifically to the concept of balance — inherent in this publishing pattern is typical of Wright, as we shall see in detail as we look at his work and career.

Though clearly and emphatically a baroque poet, Wright is more conservative stylistically than Kunitz, and for a reason noticed by Harold Segal (the scope of whose discussion, of course, does not embrace Wright). To a greater degree than Kunitz, Wright uses "variety and ornament cumulatively in support of a central unity," seeking something akin to "the Baroque vision of the indivisibility of man's world and God's." [12] While occasionally using the baroque style to playful ends, Wright maintains a deep commitment to content and theme. Kunitz uses the metaphysical style primarily in honor of occasions — the one in which the speaker's girlfriend fails to call him on the phone, for example, or the one in which the powerful change of a season makes him want to change his life.

While Wright may have known what he wanted to write about from the start of his career, it took a lot of groping and experimentation before he was able fully to express his themes. As we shall see, form is — to an unusual degree — wedded to content in his work, and it was necessary for him to discover his own unique style and form before he could truly say what was on his mind. Thus, as he himself has explained, he began by concentrating almost entirely upon style and the mechanics of writing: "when I first started writing, I was interested in the tight weave of the surface only — technique as a statement in itself, so to speak." [13] The impulse to concentrate primarily upon style — which seems not only to have carried Wright completely through his first book and well into his second but also shows up significantly in his third — was noticed by Vendler, who generalized while talking about Wright: "What above all distinguishes the true poet [is] his seeing words as things — things that make a shape on the page, things that lock together as though they had invisible hooks on them. . . . All this seeing is before and beyond any question of meaning." [14] It does indeed appear that, to discover a style that could appropriately express his subject matter, Wright first chose to experiment consciously with words, with the formal possibilities of language.

The verse in Wright's first two books seems dominated almost entirely by formal concerns; there is no readily apparent thematic continuity. The next two books, by contrast, seem to exhibit greater thematic depth and coherence. In making his selections for *Country Music*, Wright chose to republish only a few prose poems from *The Grave of the Right Hand*; each of them is distinguished by the same formal care that Hemingway is said to have lavished upon the prose experiments that make up his second book, the version of *in our time* that was issued privately in Paris in 1924. An ars poetica in Wright's second book, *Hard Freight*, indicates the almost complete exclusion of content, the singular orientation toward words, of the pieces in these first two volumes; "The New Poem" means to have little relevance to life—"It will not resemble the sea. / It will not have dirt on its thick hands"; "It will not attend our sorrow. / . . . / It will not be able to help us."

This process allowed Wright to create poems of great beauty, poems written primarily for the sake of their words, rhythms, and images. The first stanza of "White" for example—"Carafe, compotier, sea shell, vase: / Blank spaces, white objects; / Luminous knots along the black rope"—seems simply an accumulation of desirable and sometimes contrasting words and images. Such writing is certainly beautiful; what is most impressive about these lines is their attention purely to technique, to rhythms, images, and words. Elsewhere—for example in the middle stanza of "Slides of Verona"—the reader's attention is captured by something more complex, a wedding of technique to meaning through a nascent use of metaphor: "Death with its long tongue licks / Mastino's hand affection he thinks / Such sweetness such loyalty."

Interest in content seems still greater in Wright's third volume, *Bloodlines*, though even here we still find many strictly verbal experiments. The book comprises the second installment in a trilogy that begins with *Hard Freight* and concludes with *China Trace*. Wright has explained that *Bloodlines* is meant to look both backward and forward; while *Hard Freight* deals with the past and *China Trace* with the future, *Bloodlines* deals with both of these and with the present. The three volumes are also meant to be formally distinct: "I was going to have a book of separate poems and I was going to have one of longer poems, and then I was going to have a full, book-length poem." [15] Even when he does attend to content in *Bloodlines*, Wright seems more interested in abstractions than in the concrete elements inherent in his subjects. The long poems are "Tattoos" and "Skins," each composed of twenty sections of, respectively, fifteen and fourteen lines. Though "Skins" anticipates one aspect of what is to come in Wright's work—an increased interest in metaphysics, the realm on "the other side of the river"—its relentless presentation of abstractions does not at all indicate the turn toward a specific and concrete use of imagery that Wright was also to make in his later poems.

Even "Tattoos," by far the more graphic of the two sequences, is so abstract that the reader would scarcely know what was going on were it not for the brief explanatory notes appended to the sequence. ("Skins" did not have such notes when first published, though Wright added them for the reprinting in *Country Music.*) Because the notes appear separately after the poems (which do not point to them with note numbers), the first-time reader does not have even what little help they provide. Number twelve is one of the more striking and accessible installments in "Tattoos":

Oval oval oval oval push pull push pull . . .
Words unroll from our fingers.
A splash of leaves through the windowpanes,
A smell of tar from the streets:
Apple, arrival, the railroad, shoe.

The words, like bees in a sweet ink, cluster and drone,
Indifferent, indelible,
A hum and a hum:
Back stairsteps to God, ropes to the glass eye:
Vineyard, informer, the chair, the throne.

Mojo and numberless, breaths
From the wet mountains and green mouths; rustlings,
Sure sleights of hand,
The news that arrives from nowhere:
Angel, omega, silence, silence . . . .

The note for this section—"Handwriting class; Palmer Method; words as 'things'; Kingsport, Tennessee"—does make it clearer, though Wright was more generous with information when explaining the poem's occasion elsewhere:

> my real life began in the fifth grade under the all-seeing, all-knowing, all-powerful eye of Miss Grace Watkins, or "Granny Wildcat," as she was known to anyone under the age of twelve. Behind her back, of course. . . . [Her] little scholars labored to get their fingers to behave properly during penmanship lessons in the rigors of the Palmer Method. "Oval, oval, oval, oval, push, pull, push, pull" (pronounced "pursh, pull" in her solid east Tennessee accent), "rolling toward the Borden Mill, purshing toward the Peggy Anne . . ." (two, to us, very recognizable landmarks in sight of Lincoln Elementary School, one a cotton mill, the other a coffee shop).[16]

Beyond its desire to record an incident from Wright's childhood, the poem functions as an ars poetica, indicating the poet's strong interest in both language and music. Language also serves to create truth in this poem, through the words that appear mysteriously from somewhere. Wondering where they come from leads us to the other subject of the poem, its religious concern, which appropriately seems to turn the poet back on himself, God having led only from "throne" to "silence."[17]

If *Bloodlines* is Wright's most explicitly autobiographical early book, then *China Trace* is his most metaphysical. It provides an appropriate conclusion to the selected volume, for it is an unsettled book of changes, pointing as much to the future as *Bloodlines* points to the past. It is in *China Trace* that Wright comes to terms with the religious implications of the poem just quoted; as the original jacket notes for the book tell us, he investigates "identities, inherited beliefs, and assumptions once thought to be firmly acquired, that have dissolved and re-formed themselves, as rivers that change their courses alter the shape and nature of the land they nourish." Essentially what results from this process is a weakening of the religious beliefs he learned in his childhood in favor of a naturalistic humanism—though Wright's work will certainly never be free of sacramental undertones and questions, their language and imagery.

It would not be accurate to call Wright a strictly Christian poet in any of his guises, despite all the time he spent in childhood at a religiously oriented educational compound called Sky Valley ("At first, and on the outside, it was a summer camp. Later, it became a school, and all the while it was a workshop for the hammering out of little souls into the white gold of righteousness, ready for the Lord's work or the Lord's burden. . . . I spent three summers here and one entire year, in the tenth grade.") and at Christ School (eleventh and twelfth grades).[18] The closest Wright comes to mentioning Christianity is when he carefully rejects rigid theologies—for example in "1975," from *China Trace*: "At 40, the apricot / Seems raised to a higher power, the fire ant and the weed. / And I turn in the wind, / Not knowing what sign to make, or where I should kneel." Having lost the ability to pray to an unseen and abstract God, Wright turns—as these lines also demonstrate—to the natural world.[19]

The abiding and sacramental affection that Wright came to invest in the landscape is anticipated by the important (and didactic) fifth section of "Firstborn," from *Hard Freight*:

What I am trying to say
Is this—I tell you, only, the thing
That I have come to believe:

Indenture yourself to the land;
Imagine you touch its raw edges
In all weather, time and again;

Imagine its colors; try
to imitate, day by day,
The morning's growth and the dusk,

The movement of all their creatures;
Surrender yourself, and be glad;
This is the law that endures.

Wright manages to fulfill this injunction throughout his work, and he does it by locating the divine principle within nature rather than above it; as he says in

"Invisible Landscape," from *China Trace*: "God is the sleight-of-hand in the fireweed, the lost / Moment that stopped to grieve and moved on."

The final poem of the volume completes this process by offering a full definition of its title character, "Him":

His sorrow hangs like a heart in the star-flowered boundary tree.
It mirrors the endless wind.

He feeds on the lunar differences and flies up at the dawn.

When he lies down, the waters will lie down with him,
And all that walks and all that stands still, and sleep through the thunder.

It's for him that the willow bleeds.

Look for him high in the flat black of the northern Pacific sky,
Released in his suit of lights,
                              lifted and laid clear.

As the poems and passages I have been quoting make clear, there is a restrained quality to the verse in Wright's early books. It is true that a good bit of beauty here results from his dual commitment to balance (two lines, one line, two lines, one line, two lines) and precision, but it is an almost minimalist beauty, reflecting the austerity of the plain free-verse style so many American poets favored in the sixties and seventies.

Where the baroque shows in Wright's early work is in his imagery, particularly in his use of metaphor, as we see in yet another poem perhaps defining God in *China Trace*, "Dog":

The fantailed dog of the end, the lights out,
Lopes in his sleep,
The moon's moan in the glassy fields.

Everything comes to him, stone
Pad prints extending like stars, tongue black
As a flag, saliva and thread, the needle's tooth,
Everything comes to him.

If I were a wind, which I am, if I
Were smoke, which I am, if I
Were the colorless leaves, the invisible grief,
Which I am, which I am,
He'd whistle me down, and down, but not yet.

It is no idle joke to point out that *dog* is *God* spelled backwards; the poem is a much-reduced, twentieth-century (and almost certainly unintentional) rewriting of Francis Thompson's "The Hound of Heaven." Among contemporary poets, Wright and Dobyns are by far the greatest practitioners of dog imagery, though to very different ends: Wright's divine and Dobyns' elemental.

Though "Dog" is baroque in its use of metaphor, it still appears restrained when viewed from the perspective of Wright's later work—not that we had long to wait for that more mature style to begin appearing. Even before the publication of *Country Music* Wright had already published his fifth volume, *The Southern Cross*, where we find the extraordinarily baroque, descriptive "Dog Day Vespers":

Sun like an orange mousse through the trees,
A snowfall of trumpet bells on the oleander;
                                        mantis paws
Craning out of the new wisteria; fruit smears in the west . . .
DeStael knifes a sail on the bay;
A mother's summons hangs like a towel on the dusk's hook.

Everything drips and spins
In the pepper trees, the pastel glide of the evening

Slowing to mother-of-pearl and the night sky.
Venus breaks clear in the third heaven.
Quickly the world is capped, and the seal turned.

I drag my chair to the deck's edge and the blue ferns.
I'm writing you now by flashlight,
The same news and the same story I've told you often before.
As the stag-stars begin to shine,
A wing brushes my left hand,

> but it's not my wing.

How deeply and traditionally baroque this poem is is demonstrated in the fact that Harold Segal seems to have discussed — many years before Wright composed his poem — both its theme and its imagery in a general comment on the use of light in baroque poetry:

> In the Baroque . . . the light source is seldom bright sun but the warm orange-hued glow of later afternoon or the reddish sky of dawn or sunset; instead of coming from above diffusing all beneath it in a uniform brightness, as in the Renaissance, the light now enters from a side, leaving large areas obscured by darkness or semidarkness. This, complemented by an opposition of light and dark, suggested no longer the clear sense of certitude of Renaissance man but instead the Baroque cognizance of a spiritual realm yet inextricably bound up with the terrestrial, and the Baroque fondness for the dramatic.[20]

Often what a baroque poem describes is surprisingly simple, considering the amount of energy that is expended in the telling of it. "Dog Day Vespers" really does little more than describe the onslaught of sunset as viewed from a deck above Laguna Beach, California. The poem contains images galore but is in no sense merely imagistic. Image is wound upon image, simile upon simile, metaphor upon metaphor; nothing is given to us straight, everything is doubled and tripled. At the end the poem takes a final leap also mentioned by Segal; not only does the image of the wing allude to Dante — Wright's favorite source of sacramental meaning — it also expresses the speaker's baroque sense of a spiritual imminence lying within the glory of the physical world.

Which would seem to be the most important thematic news presented in Wright's books since *China Trace*, the volumes gathered in *The World of the Ten Thousand Things*. These volumes are indeed closely related in terms of theme, but they are even more closely related in terms of methodology. In fact, in an important sense their theme is their methodology, or vice versa — an idea that Wright has himself expressed in an only slightly veiled and fragmented way. When Carol Ellis asked him about a statement he had once made about Philip Larkin's concept of form, Wright said: "Larkin's comment was 'Form means nothing to me. Content is everything.' My comment would be that content means nothing to me. Form is everything. Which is to say, to me the most vital question in poetry is the question of form." Expanding upon this later in the interview, Wright connected form to content at its deepest level: "As Roethke said, 'I long for the quietness at the heart of form.' Well, he doesn't mean 'forms.' He doesn't mean a sonnet. He means Form. Organization. The secret of the universe is Form, even if poems are not the secret of the universe. They're only clues to the secret of the universe."[21]

By expanding both the size of his poems and the length of his lines, Wright took a quantum leap in *The Southern Cross* toward the kind of form he seems always to have been pursuing. As he has told the story, Wright found the solution to the fact that he "was never able to get a grip on narrative (and still can't to this day)" in Ezra Pound's *Personae*: "the lyric poem that was structured associationally, not narratively."[22] Imagery is the element of poetry that is of most use to Wright in this type of poem for the way imagery allows him to expand the scope of his vision: "If one of the true functions of poetry is a contemplation of the divine, as I believe it is, and if writing poems is my way of doing that, as it comes increasingly to be, then my ability to think imagistically can turn out to be a great relief to me, rather than the grief I had previously thought it whenever I tried to tell a story."[23] Wright uses imagery to describe landscapes, to develop atmospheres, and to recount incidents and events from his own life, from history, and from literature.

Like *Bloodlines*, *The Southern Cross* is a book of memory. Time, its most pervasive concern, appears both in a preoccupation with death and in a preoccupation with memory and the burden of the past. Its best poems are the two long ones that open and close it. Each of the eight pages of "Homage to Paul Cézanne" contains an untitled and unnumbered section; all of them focus upon the dead and try to tell how the dead interact with the living and are present to us now — particularly through poems and paintings. In the fourth of these sections Wright most clearly connects the dead with the paintings of Cézanne:

> The dead are a cadmium blue.
> We spread them with palette knives in broad blocks and planes.
>
> We layer them stroke by stroke
> In steps and ascending mass, in verticals raised from the earth.
>
> We choose, and layer them in,
> Blue and a blue and a breath,
>
> Circle and smudge, cross-beak and buttonhook,
> We layer them in. We squint hard and terrace them line by line.
>
> And so we are come between, and cry out,
> And stare up at the sky and its cloudy panes,
>
> And finger the cypress twists.
> The dead understand all this, and keep in touch,
>
> Rustle of hand to hand in the lemon trees,
> Flags, and the great sifts of anger
>
> To powder and nothingness.
> The dead are a cadmium blue, and they understand.

In the first section of the poem, Wright relates language and poetry to the dead by saying that "Like us, / They keep on saying the same thing, trying to get it right"; in the eighth and last section he ties Cézanne, poetry, language, and the dead together in images drawn from this fourth section:

What we are given in dreams we write as blue paint,
Or messages to the clouds.
At evening we wait for the rain to fall and the sky to clear.
Our words are words for the clay, uttered in undertones,
Our gestures salve for the wind.

In section four it is the logic and progression of the images that is perhaps most interesting. The presentation of the dead through the action of painting is perfectly clear through the fifth line, though it does sound as though the clouds in this painting must be blue since the "cadmium blue" dead are described as having the shape of clouds. "Cross-beak and buttonhook" in line six are used associatively and metaphorically since they have nothing to do either with the act of painting or with clouds. In line seven, poetry is allied with painting as the dead are terraced "line by line." A neat connection is made when the speaker fingers "the cypress twists" and the dead "keep in touch" through the rustling of the leaves of the lemon trees, which seem to be comprised of their hands. The section is more oblique than precise, as befits its subject; it presents a feeling of the presence of the dead rather than actual knowledge of them.

When Dobyns writes of the dead in *Cemetery Nights* he treats them in strictly physical terms, as bodies gradually rotting and drying to dust. Though he does suggest that the presence of the dead may occasionally be felt in a gust of wind or in dust motes hanging in the air of a still room, these appearances are ascribed not to any vision of truth but to the imaginations of characters in the poems. Wright is also careful to locate his hints of the presence of the dead in natural phenomena, but he does not distance these hints from himself. While Dobyns, writing from his perspective of depressed realism, scorns any notion of an afterlife, Wright's baroque sensibility allows him to suggest, coyly and only through imagery and metaphor, a mingling of the here and the hereafter.[24]

The final and title poem of the volume, "The Southern Cross," is less concerned with death than with memory and the burdens of a personal past, just as the title refers less to the constellation than to the cherished burden of Wright's Tennessee heritage and his preoccupation with Italy (southern in a European context), both of which define him, establishing the "cross" he carries through his life. The poem is rich in image and incident, with interspersed passages of a more abstract nature. Wright has explained that for him the American South represents the fecundity of earth, a purely physical beauty, while Italy represents the spiritual: "Italy is metaphysical."[25] Like the entire book, this poem attempts to unite these two realms not just as parts of the poet's past, his memory, but also — and more importantly — as concepts. The poem ends with him wishing he could completely reinhabit the world of the South as it existed at the time of his birth:

> It's what we forget that defines us, and stays in the same place,
> And waits to be rediscovered.
> Somewhere in all that network of rivers and roads and silt hills,
> A city I'll never remember,
>   its walls the color of pure light,
> Lies in the August heat of 1935,
> In Tennessee, the bottom land slowly becoming a lake.
> It lies in a landscape that keeps my imprint
> Forever,
>   and stays unchanged, and waits to be filled back in.
> Someday I'll find it out
> And enter my old outline as though for the 1st time,
>
> And lie down, and tell no one.

The odd promise to tell no one so hard-won a truth, were it to be discovered, has a profound rightness at the conclusion of this poem: throughout the poem and the book, it is not the finding that concerns Wright but the searching. We recall that the constellation, the Southern Cross, is a navigational aid to travelers, but of course it is not visible from the northern hemisphere. It seems clear, then, that Wright has structured this questing poem in a fundamentally uncertain way, so that it cannot arrive at its destination; his emphasis is consistently upon events and objects that are not at hand, that cannot quite be remembered.

The Other Side of the River continues the formal breakthrough toward expansive form achieved in *The Southern Cross*; most of the poems tend to run on for several pages each. *The Other Side of the River* makes use of four basic settings or locales. California is the setting of the present moment, the present tense, the time of actual speaking. Memory carries the speaker into the past, which has two generalized settings — Italy and the American South. Desire carries him toward the future, into imagination or vision, the hint of salvation, whose domain is set across the river. The title Wright has chosen for this book seems intentionally to echo the title of one of James Wright's books, *Shall We Gather at the River*—in which a poem called "Willy Lyons" imagines the speaker's uncle as having achieved peace after his death by crossing the river— the River Styx masquerading as the Ohio River. In his title poem, Charles Wright's speaker expresses his wish in this way: "I want to sit by the bank of the river, / in the shade of the evergreen tree, / And look in the face of whatever, / the whatever that's waiting for me." [26] Perhaps it is the pat use of rhyme here that makes us doubt the ultimate truth of this vision; Charles Wright never explicitly accepts transcendence in his poems, however much otherworldly desire he expresses. As Bruce Bond has said, both the desire and the limitations are based on Wright's use of imagery: "In spite of their longing for transcendence, Wright's poems remain forcefully visual, as if the image were both bridge and barrier to the unseen, the most immediate objects assuming a metaphysical inscrutability and allure." [27]

Despite the fact that they contain elements that are clearly narrative, Wright's most characteristic poems are dominantly meditative and circular. Rather than tell stories, they incorporate incidents and events into imagistic structures that contemplate matters deserving of serious thought; the author or his speaker gradually circles in on the truth. In the words of Vendler: "[Wright's] synoptic and panoramic vision, radiating out from a compositional center to a filled canvas, opposes itself to the anthropocentric, and consequently autobiographical or narrative, impetus of lyrics with a linear base."[28] The opening poem of *The Other Side of the River* illustrates this meditative circularity; "Lost Bodies" is divided into seven unnumbered sections, each performing a specific function. The first section is introductory, much as the first sections of so many of Whitman's open-form poems are introductory. And just as Whitman so often does, Wright introduces all of the elements of his poem briefly at the start:

> Last night I thought of Torri del Benaco again,
> Its almond trees in blossom,
>   its cypresses clothed in their dark fire,
>
> And the words carved on that concrete cross
>
> I passed each day of my life
> In Kingsport going to town
>   GET RIGHT WITH GOD / JESUS IS COMING SOON.
>
> If I had it all to do over again
>   I'd be a Medievalist.
> I'd thoroughly purge my own floor.
>
> Something's for sure in the clouds, but it's not for me,
>
> Though all the while that light tips the fast-moving water,
> East wind in a rush through the almond trees.

The first three lines introduce the Italian setting that forms the basis for one of the poem's patterns of memory; the next four lines introduce the setting in the American South that is the basis for the other pattern. The concluding six lines are thematic. The desire to be a medievalist seems like a wish for certainty, perhaps religious certainty. The something that is "for sure in the clouds" may suggest a spiritual possibility—the efficacy of which the speaker immediately denies but then just as quickly seems to grant, though in a different form: if he cannot find the spiritual in the clouds, perhaps he can find it in the more earthbound light on the water and wind in the trees.

The following six sections of the poem establish a regular and repetitive pattern: numbers two and five develop the memory of Tennessee; three and six develop the memory of Italy; four and seven develop the theme, the meanings of these memories. Charles Wright grew up in Tennessee; after college he lived in Italy while serving in the United States Army. The sense of spirituality that is developed in the Tennessee sections is earthy and Christian, the word emphatically made flesh: "the cross is still there, sunk deeper into the red clay / Than anyone could have set it." Wright has provided an indirect gloss on these passages in "Lonesome Pine Special," where he asserts: "In the world of dirt, each tactile thing / repeats the untouchable / In its own way, and in its own time." [29]

Spirituality in the Italian sections is more evanescent, not so much inherent within material objects as dancingly associated with them; it exists in the interplay between wind, water, and vegetation:

An east wind was blowing out toward the water . . .

I remember the cypress nods in its warm breath.
I remember the almond blossoms
                    floating out on the waves, west to Salò.
I remember the way they looked there,
                    a small flotilla of matches.

I remember their flash in the sun's flare.

The thematic sections are rational and intellectual rather than emotional and imagistic; though a desire for belief, for faith, seems expressed in them, it is overridden by the logic of doubt: "You've got to sign your name to something, it seems to me. / And so we rephrase the questions / Endlessly, / hoping the answer might somehow change." The answer the speaker wishes would change is that taught by the facts of everyday life:

When you die, you fall down,
                              you don't rise up
Like a scrap of burnt paper into the everlasting.
Each morning we learn this painfully,
        pulling our bodies up by the roots from their deep sleep.

No matter how hard he strives to make them suffice, the speaker of these poems ultimately cannot rest easy with the limited religious answers he considers.

Both the questions and the answers, the images and the statements, the doubts and the longings, however, are expressed in language, and language is always the underlying subject of Wright's poems. In "To Giacomo Leopardi in the Sky," Wright asserts the spiritual function of words while questioning their efficacy:

Not one word has ever melted in glory not one.
We keep on sending them up, however,
As the sun rains down.
                          You did it yourself,
All those nights looking up at the sky, wanting to be there
Away from the grief of being here
In the wrong flesh.
They must look funny to you now,
Rising like smoke signals into the infinite,
The same letter over and over,
                          big o and little o.

If words cannot reach as far as heaven, then the solution Wright seeks in these poems must only exist as a component of poetry itself; somehow the form of the search is its own mysterious answer. Wright's thinking is circular indeed, as the search for an answer so often brings us and him back to the starting point at the end. Thus when he asserts what seems an ultimate answer in "California Dreaming," we end up back where we started: "What I know best is a little thing. / It sits on the far side of the simile, / the like that's like the like." The statement does not express belief in a settled truth; it establishes a path, a method, which might lead to some sense of truth—if spiritual certainty is to be found, that is, it will be discovered through the operations of something like metaphor or simile. The similarity of this to what we found to be the ultimate aim of Simic's poetry—to touch the deepest element of *being* through the use of metaphor—is certainly striking. The two poets are close friends; their correspondence on the uses of imagery in poetry was published in the *Gettysburg Review* in 1995.[30]

Even more obviously to the point of Wright's work is a passage from the title poem in *The Other Side of the River*, where Wright comments directly upon the meditative, metaphorical, circular method of his long poems:

It's linkage I'm talking about,
                    and harmonies and structures
And all the various things that lock our wrists to the past.

Something infinite behind everything appears,
                    and then disappears.

It's all a matter of how
                    you narrow the surfaces.
It's all a matter of how you fit in the sky.

Wright is talking neither about reality nor about settled truth here; his subject is the method of his poetry, the process whereby truth might someday be cajoled to reveal itself out of the confusing, the camouflaging, the byzantine fabric of the reality that conceals it.

The expansion of form that Wright began with *The Southern Cross* and continued with *The Other Side of the River* took another small leap forward in his next volume, *Zone Journals.* These journal poems are even less committed to tidy notions of structure than the poems that come before them. The new pattern is continued into *Xionia,* which contains another fifteen journal poems. Still, these two books are far more similar stylistically to the earlier books than they are dissimilar; in terms of theme we also find the latest poems similar to the ones immediately preceding them, as Wright continues to explore the relationship between the physical and the spiritual realms. And, again as before, his starting point and emphasis is with concrete images of reality; the holiness must trail after — like the shadow of a waving branch playing among fallen leaves.

In *Zone Journals* Wright is not particularly coy about what he is searching for; in the second poem he creates an image that lays out his theme:

> One of those weightless, effortless late September days
> As sycamore leaves
>   tack down the unresisting air
> Onto the fire-knots of late roses
> Still pumping their petals of flame
>   up from the English loam,
> And I suddenly recognize
> The difference between the spirit and flesh
>   is finite, and slowly transgressable.

Wright wishes to demonstrate the presence of the spiritual within the realm of the real, and his approach is like that of the English rose: to grow from the soil, rich and real, to reach tentatively into the air, vague and insubstantial, and to produce a miracle of transubstantial beauty at the end of an extended stem. That's all.[31]

Nearly at the geographical center of this book we find a curious passage in which a departed, elder sage bestows upon the acolyte poet his sense of mission. The figurative imagery of Wright's framing is both entertaining and baroque:

Who is it here in the night garden,
                              gown a transparent rose
Down to his ankles, great sleeves
Spreading the darkness around him wherever he steps,
Laurel corona encircling his red transparent headcap, . . .
                    voice like a slow rip through silk cloth
In disapproval? *Brother*, he says, pointing insistently,
A sound of voices starting to turn in the wind and then disappear as
      though
Orbiting us, *Brother, remember the way it was*
In my time: nothing has changed:
Penitents terrace the mountainside, the stars hang in their bright courses
And darkness is still the dark:
                              concentrate, listen hard,
Look to the nature of all things.

The insistent, fatherly saint — of course Dante, come to guide the younger poet
as Virgil came to guide Dante — is himself a rose, growing from the soil of the
grave. Look and listen, he says — look to the spiritual heart of "all things";
listen for the unutterable sound:

In the rings and after-chains,
In the great river of language that circles the universe,
Everything comes together, . . .
                    there is a word, one word,
For each of us, circling and holding fast
In all that cascade and light.
Said once, or said twice,
                    it gathers and waits its time to come back
To its true work:
                    concentrate, listen hard.

Wright will deal more fully with the subject of language in *Xionia*; here he prefers to concentrate upon objects — real, visible, audible. Moreover, he does not specify precisely the nature of the spiritual center that he seeks; in fact, his aesthetic requires that he *not* specify it. He speaks of "the obvious end of art" as being "that grace / Beyond its reach" and asserts that "what's outside / The picture is more important than what's in." Form and content thus correspond wonderfully to one another in *Zone Journals*, as each requires that there be an unspoken heart to the utterance. But because the spiritual is inherent within the physical and not separate from it, it does not subtract from what is here. Instead, it lies just beneath the surface or just off the page, energizing what we are given.

The baroque is present everywhere in these poems — in Wright's lush musicality, in his rich use of imagery and metaphor, and in the linkage of the invisible realm of spirit to the visible realm of reality. Thus the unseen adds energy to the seen, twisting it from its axis, enriching its colors and forms. Here is Wright describing the night in typical form:

> The stars are fastening their big buckles
> and flashy night shoes,
> Thunder chases its own tail down the sky,
> My forty-ninth year, and all my Southern senses called to horn,
> August night hanging like cobwebs around my shoulders:
> How existential it all is, really,
> the starting point always the starting point
> And what's-to-come still being the What's-to-Come.
> Some friends, like George, lurk in the memory like locusts,
> while others, flat one-sided fish
> Looking up, handle themselves like sweet stuff:
> look out for them, look out for them.

It is not just the oddness of the individual images here that is baroque but the unharmonious profusion of odd images. Although Dr. Johnson recognized that the metaphysical poets of the seventeenth century wished to yoke "the most heterogeneous ideas . . . by violence together" through a kind of *discordia concors*, he ended up finding more *discordia* than *concors*.[32] So it is with this passage. When the speaker finds his senses "called to horn," we suspect that he has been awakened to a fox hunt, or perhaps just to another day in boot camp. These possibilities might be said to be reinforced by the first image, in which the nighttime revelers seem to be gathering themselves for home. The description of the threatening morning sky, however, is ornamental, as must be the concluding images — unless we decide that the quarry of the speaker is not foxes but insects or fish. The ultimate meaning of these lines remains mysterious, but not the importance of the search, the necessity that the speaker "look out for them."

Metaphysical and baroque poets have always been susceptible to the charge of mixing their metaphors, and certainly Wright does not escape his share of the guilt. Indeed, the very aspect of Wright's work that most obviously defines his style is — as we might expect — also the aspect of his work that is most controversial among critics. Robert Pinsky, for example, suggests that "Often Wright's style is so clotted with figures of speech . . . that everything else tends to vanish."[33] X. J. Kennedy, a sympathetic reader of Wright's poems, has pointed to extreme metaphors that he finds both successful and unsuccessful: "As always, Wright has a rare way with a metaphor: 'Spring picks the locks of the wind,' 'The reindeer still file through the bronchial trees.' Still, he is not always discriminate, as in lines about bears (the constellations) 'serene as black coffee,' and about 'Sun like an orange mousse.'"[34] There are no laws where taste is concerned; Kennedy's last negative example has already appeared among my positive ones.

Similarly, one of the metaphors praised by Kennedy is ridiculed in this comment made by Mary Kinzie: "Some of [Wright's] personifications are quite funny: 'Spring picks the locks of the wind'; 'spaces / In black shoes, their hands clasped'; 'The dead are constant in / The white lips of the sea.' Some of the stage props the dead must carry around are also awkwardly amusing: 'We filagree and we baste. / But what do the dead care for the fringe of words, / Safe in their suits of milk?'"[35] Calvin Bedient begins his critique of Wright's use of extreme metaphor by commenting on lines from the poem "Vesper Journal" ("petals fall like tiny skirts / From the dogwood tree next door, / last things in the last light"): "Charming as they may be, those 'tiny skirts' need to be shipped back to the warehouse; they're frivolous in the neighborhood of 'last things.' . . . Again, does it signify, in 'Language Journal,' that the light is 'cantaloupe-colored'? Is this any more than a 'pretty' detail? To call such luscious light 'Light of martyrs and solitaries' only makes matters worse, as does imagining it 'ladled' like 'a liquid' on the trees." Curiously, this is the same critic who begins his review with this praise of Wright's baroque sensibility: "Through his startling figures and, if less so, his eloquent rhythms, he has intimated an unthinkable glory of which life is otherwise bereft." [36] This last statement, of course, echoes my own thinking.

The ten poems that make up *Zone Journals* are geographically expansive, ranging from California to Italy to England, and with many scenes set in Virginia. The poems are linear in the way they handle time, with many of the sections in each dated and chronologically arranged. In terms of meaning, however, the poems are accretive, speculative, and ruminative; they do not move forward from a beginning to a middle and an end. The central poem, "A Journal of the Year of the Ox," proceeds entirely through 1985; the entry for May 15 is typical for the way it mixes concrete imagery of spring with thoughts on the nature of existence:

> — In the first inch of afternoon, under the peach trees,
> The constellations of sunlight
> Sifting along their courses among the posed limbs,
> It's hard to imagine the north wind
>   wishing us ill,
> Revealing nothing at all and wishing us ill
> In God's third face.
>   The world is an ampersand,
> And I lie in sweet clover,
>   bees like golden earrings
> Dangling and locked fast to its white heads,
> Watching the clouds move and the constellations of

light move
Through the trees, as they both will
When the wind weathers them on their way,
When the wind weathers them to that point
                    where all things meet.

The goal of this volume is to speculate about that point, where the seen and the unseen might come together and reinforce one another. However, Wright still does not quite seem confident about where that occurs and how it might be achieved. Discovering and revealing that is the task he undertakes in *Xionia*.

Whereas the structure of *Zone Journals* is chronological and accretive, that of *Xionia* is symmetrical. Placed at the center of the fifteen poems in *Xionia* is the eighth of them, "Language Journal." Immediately preceding and following it are "Primitive Journal" and "Primitive Journal II," the latter of which answers the former. Similarly, poem ten, the optimistic "May Journal," answers poem six, the pessimistic "Georg Trakl Journal," and poem twelve, "A Journal of Southern Rivers," provides the thematic climax anticipated in poem four, "December Journal." The first three poems are introductory and the final three consolidate the gains made in number twelve. Finally, the poems alternate in length, with the odd numbered poems being short and the even numbered poems being long. Wright has always favored balanced patterns; in interviews he is forever identifying the exact centers of poems, sequences, and books.

Xionia is both about truth and about poetry. Wright wishes to express wisdom about the nature of the universe, particularly how it integrates the spiritual and the physical, at the same time as he wishes to understand how this expression, this complicated use of words, can occur. Because of the way in which the two interact with one another, Wright is as interested in the nature of language as he is in the substance of truth. Richard Jackson has commented on this aspect of Wright's work:

> In the context of an Idealistic Neo-Confucianism, Wright's world becomes one of presences that are inadequate substitutes for the absence he desires. As a result, the objects of his landscape aspire to the condition of language,

our substitute, if we can trust the linguistic critics (Jacques Lacan, for example), for what we cannot fully possess, for what is missing. In a roundabout way, he hopes language will bring him the void, will allow him to become, as another epigraph suggests, "an emblem among emblems." [37]

As is so often the case in his writings, Wright begins the sequence of poems that makes up *Xionia* with a kind of hypothesis:

> Inaudible consonant, inaudible vowel
> The word continues to fall
>   in splendor around us
> Window half shadow window half moon
>   back yard like a book of snow
> That holds nothing and that nothing holds
> Immaculate text
>   not too prescient not too true.

Wright's two subjects — truth and articulation — are brought together here, as in the sequence as a whole, through an identification of nature with language. Wright suggests that the most crucial utterances may occur not only within poems but also within the sacred and visible world of nature.

In the central poem "Language Journal" Wright considers the relationship between language and reality. As is often his strategy, he first presents a false viewpoint — in this case the contention of "the theorists" that "everything comes from language": "Nothing means anything, the slip of phrase against phrase / Contains the real way our lives / Are graphed out and understood, / the transformation of adverb / To morpheme and phoneme is all we need answer to" — and then disagrees with it: "But I don't think so today." Wright goes on to assert that language is conduit, not creator, of truth: "Whatever it is, the language is only its moan. / Whatever it is, the self's trace / lingers along it." Abstraction is not truth; without the real to give it form and substance (concepts that together yield utterance), abstraction has no being.

"December Journal," the fourth poem in the sequence, uses the same strategy of false statement followed by a correction to nearly the same end, beginning:

> God is not offered to the senses,
> St. Augustine tells us,
> The artificer is not his work, but is his art:
> Nothing is good if it can be better.
> But all these oak trees look fine to me . . . .

Wright takes this occasion to praise the complexities of the physical world, which he is convinced embodies the abstractions within it:

> I keep coming back to the visible.
> I keep coming back
> To what it leads me into,
> The hymn in the hymnal,
> The object, sequence and consequence.
> By being exactly what it is,
> It is that other, inviolate self we yearn for,
> Itself and more than itself,
> the word inside the word.
> It is the tree and what the tree stands in for, the blank,
> The far side of the last equation.

In an interview, Wright commented upon the directness of his journal poems, how they allow him to say exactly what he thinks: "They are more didactic than other poems, perhaps, and more emotionally open. One tends to speak one's mind more nakedly in journals. One tends to say what is really troubling one's sleep."[38] Certainly in these lines, and throughout *Xionia*, Wright wants to be sure we understand his meaning.

   Wright feels, most emphatically, the presence of the truth that he seeks within nature itself, which seems to *speak* to him. In "May Journal" — tenth in the series and the one corresponding to "December Journal"—he senses this truth most strongly, but is still unable fully to articulate it:

What is it in all myth
                    that brings us back from the dead?
What is it that jump-starts in verisimilitude
And ends up in ecstacy,
That takes us by both hands
                    from silence to speechlessness?
What is it that brings us out of the rock with such pain,
As though the sirens had something to say to us after all
From their clover and green shore,
                    the words of their one song
Translatable, note by note?
As though the inexpressible were made inexpressible.

It is in such a passage as this that Wright most resembles Robert Penn Warren. In his wonderful late volume *Being Here* (1980), as sporadically throughout his mature career, Warren also sought to understand the truth that he felt was being uttered by nature. His poem "Code Book Lost," for example, begins:

What does the veery say, at dusk in shad-thicket?
There must be some meaning, or why should your heart stop,

As though, in the dark depth of water, Time held its breath,
While the message spins on like a spool of silk thread fallen?

The uncertainty that Wright feels is echoed at the end of Warren's poem: "Yes, message on message, like wind or water, in light or in dark, / The whole world pours at us. But the code book, somehow, is lost." [39]

Wright comes to his answer in the twelfth poem of *Xionia*, "A Journal of Southern Rivers," which begins by positing a question—"*What hast thou, O my soul, with Paradise*"—we seem to have heard before. This is yet another way of asking, What is the ultimate relationship between the unseen and the seen, the spiritual and the physical? The answer comes in another passage that refers to a figure of authority, but this time a figure whose position is not undercut:

> If being is Being, as Martin Heidegger says,
> There is no other question,
> > nothing to answer to,
> That's worth the trouble.
> In awe and astonishment we regain ourselves in this world.
> There is no other.

Since there is no other world, no spiritual realm that is separate from the physical realm in which we live our lives, then the poet can truly immerse himself in both realms by living fully in this one. Ultimately it is the ongoing process — of language, of poetry, of life — that captures his attention, rather than the finished product of a spiritual realm waiting at the end. Spirituality is to be found in poems.

Among contemporary American poets, Wright would seem to be the one who most fulfills the characteristics of the baroque mode. Not only does he write — musically, imagistically, and metaphorically — in the strikingly lush style that we call baroque, but he does so with real substance, habitually searching for signs of the spiritual within the physical, the unseen within the seen. It also happens that he is conscious of doing this, as is evident from a comment that he made almost offhandedly to J. D. McClatchy: "One more thing. Some years ago Octavio Paz called for what I seem to remember as a 'Baroque-abstract' in painting. A kind of Mannerism. A non-pejorative Mannerism. I think that has happened in the work, say, of Frank Stella. I think it is also happening, here and there, in poetry. One could name names — Ashbery, for instance. It is a position that interests me as well." [40]

Except for Kunitz, Wright is more different from the other poets considered in this book than he is similar to them. And yet there are areas of similarity. When he mentions Ashbery in his comment on a nonpejorative mannerism just above, for example, Wright is pointing to one of these similarities: Ashbery and Wright both write their poems at a far edge of contemporary style, the edge that favors floridness, curlicues, and complicated thinking. With Simic, Wright shares an interest in extreme linkages of imagery, in far-ranging uses of metaphor; indeed for both poets this type of figuration is crucial to philosophical understanding. With Stern, Wright shares an interest in the sacredness of things, the wonders of nature. With Dobyns, however, he seems to share almost nothing, beyond the fact that they are both contemporary American poets.

What makes Wright most unique within this group is his attitude, or non-attitude, toward most aspects of life in the twentieth century: he rarely if ever refers to politics; he does not describe massacres, atrocities, drive-by shootings, muggings; he seems relatively unbothered by the prospect of certain death. Though Ashbery is somewhat less grounded in explicit details of twentieth-century life than Dobyns, Simic, or Stern, Wright seems much less grounded in them than Ashbery. In almost every way we can think of he is the least time-bound of these poets, the one most comfortable with a style and way of thinking inherited from the seventeenth century. And yet he still lacks the sense of certainty we see in the earlier baroque artists; though he asks many of the same questions as they, he arrives at no certain set of answers, no settled core of beliefs. Rather, his questions lead him to shadows and hints, desires and longings, evanescent scenarios more likely to have emanated from his own imagination than from the world of reality. Because of the relentlessly questioning nature of Wright's religious seeking, we can see working in him, too, the principle of uncertainty.

Notes

INTRODUCTION

1. DeFrees' essay, "Resolution and Independence: John Berryman and the Meaning of Life," appears in the *Gettysburg Review* (Winter 1996), 9–29.

2. My experiences with John Berryman's skills as a teacher are recounted in my essay "John Berryman: His Teaching, His Scholarship, His Poetry," in *Recovering Berryman: Essays on a Poet*, ed. Richard J. Kelly and Alan K. Lathrop (Ann Arbor: University of Michigan Press, 1993), 43–56.

3. In his book *The Cosmic Code: Quantum Physics as the Language of Nature*, physicist Heinz Pagels applies this understanding back to the macrophysical world: "Science shows us that the visible world is neither matter nor spirit; the visible world is the invisible organization of energy" (New York: Bantam Books, 1982), 312.

4. Pagels, 67–68. For humanist readers who are interested in this topic, I would like to recommend two additional sources. The first is the entry "Quantum Mechanics, Philosophical Implications of," by Norwood Russell Hanson, in *The Encyclopedia of Philosophy*, vol. 7, ed. Paul Edwards (New York: Macmillan & Free Press, 1967), 41–49. On the death of determinism, Hanson (a philosopher) says: "Such rules as do structure quantum mechanics run clearly counter to any metaphysical preconceptions familiar to philosophers with a nineteenth-century outlook. Therefore, it becomes a reasonable metaphysical possibility that nature is fundamentally indeterministic; that elementary particles are, ontologically, always in partially defined states; that they do not in any sense that is scientifically respectable and philosophically intelligible have both a precise position and an exact energy" (46).

   The other source is one that I will be referring to several times in my argument to come; although it was written almost seventy years ago, P. G. Bridgman's article "The New Vision of Science" is — according to Robert P. Crease and Charles C. Mann, authors of *The Second Creation: Makers of the Revolution in 20th-Century Physics* (New York: Macmillan, 1986), 71 — an "exposition of quantum mechanics for the nonphysicist as good as any that has been published in the intervening six decades." Bridgman defines the death of determinism in a somewhat different way, by pointing out that "The same situation confronts the physicist everywhere; whenever he penetrates to the atomic or electronic level in his analysis, he finds things acting in a way for which he can assign no cause, for which he never can assign a cause, and for which the concept of cause has no meaning, if Heisenberg's principle is right" (*Harper's* [March 1929], 448).

Many excellent books have been written on this subject for general readers. I do think that Pagels gives the best account, and the book by Crease and Mann mentioned above is excellent. I also recommend *In Search of Shrödinger's Cat* by John Gribbin (New York: Bantam Books, 1984), *Quantum Reality* by Nick Herbert (Garden City: Anchor/Doubleday, 1985), *Taking the Quantum Leap* by Fred Alan Wolf (San Francisco: Harper & Row, 1981), *The Structure of Scientific Revolutions* by Thomas S. Kuhn (Chicago: University of Chicago Press, 1962; 1970), and *Quantum Profiles* by Jeremy Bernstein (Princeton: Princeton University Press, 1991). Two somewhat more fanciful but still interesting books are *The Tao of Physics* by Fritjof Capra (New York: Bantam Books, 1977) and *The Dancing Wu Li Masters* by Gary Zukav (New York: William Morrow, 1979). Another essential text is *Physics and Philosophy* by Werner Heisenberg (New York: Harper & Row, 1958), though readers should certainly not begin their studies with it.

5. The first quote is from Pagels, 69; the second and third are from Pagels, 76.
6. Pagels, 73.
7. Bridgman, 446.
8. Charles Simic, "Negative Capability and Its Children," in *The Uncertain Certainty: Interviews, Essays and Notes on Poetry* (Ann Arbor: University of Michigan Press, 1985), 91.

JOHN ASHBERY

1. Robert Boyers, "A Quest without an Object," *Times Literary Supplement* (1 September 1978), 962. After quoting these sentiments, Marjorie Perloff replied in exasperation: "This is to regard *meaning* as some sort of fixed quantity (like two pounds of sugar or a dozen eggs) that the poet as speaker can either 'leave out' or proffer to the expectant auditor with whom he is engaged in 'shared discourse'" (*The Poetics of Indeterminacy: Rimbaud to Cage* [Princeton: Princeton University Press, 1981], 255).
2. See Lieberman's "John Ashbery: Unassigned Frequencies: Whispers Out of Time," in his *Unassigned Frequencies: American Poetry in Review, 1964–1977* (Urbana: University of Illinois Press, 1977), 3–61.

3. David Shapiro, *John Ashbery: An Introduction to the Poetry* (New York: Columbia University Press, 1979), 17.

4. Gustave Flaubert, "Letter to Louise Colst (1852)," *Selected Letters*, trans. Francis Steegmuller (New York: Farrar, Straus & Giroux, 1954), 127–28.

5. John Ashbery, "The Impossible," *Poetry* 90.4 (July 1957), 251.

6. Dana Gioia, "Poetry Chronicle," *Hudson Review* 34 (1981–1982), 588–89.

7. John Ashbery, review of *Weathers and Edges, New York Herald Tribune Book World* 3.42 (4 September 1966), 2.

8. Davide Fite, "On the Virtues of Modesty: John Ashbery's Tactics against Transcendence," *Modern Language Quarterly* 42 (1981), 78–79.

9. Shapiro, 10.

10. Shapiro, xiv.

11. Peter Stitt, "The Art of Poetry XXXIII: John Ashbery," *Paris Review* 90 (Winter 1983), 44–45.

12. John Frederick Nims, ed., *The Harper Anthology of Poetry* (New York: Harper & Row, 1981), 770.

13. Peter Hainsworth, "Change Unchanging," *Times Literary Supplement* (21 December 1984), 1466.

14. Ashbery, in A. Poulin, Jr., "The Experience of Experience: A Conversation with John Ashbery," *Michigan Quarterly Review* 20 (1981), 245.

15. Stitt, 43, 49.

16. Thomas A. Fink, "The Comic Thrust of Ashbery's Poetry," *Twentieth Century Literature* 30 (1984), 8. We must never forget that Ashbery is a very funny poet; indeed, Robert Miklitsch believes that, "Despite evidence to the contrary, . . . Ashbery's great unacknowledged gift is his sense of humor. . . . Often, when a poem seems on the brink of disaster, Ashbery's comic strain flashes like a Chaplinesque gesture to transform apparent catastrophe into a *coup de maître*" ("John Ashbery," *Contemporary Literature* 21 [1980], 131).

17. During our interview, I asked Ashbery about "the way the details of a poem will be so clear, but the context, the surrounding situation, unclear. Perhaps this is more a matter of perspective than any desire to befuddle." He replied: "This is the way that life appears to me, the way that experience happens. I can concentrate on the things in this room and our talking together, but what the context is is mysterious to me. And it's not that I want to make it more mysterious in my poems — really, I just want to make it more photographic" (Stitt, 43).

18. David Spurr, "John Ashbery's Poetry of Language," *Centennial Review* 25 (1981), 152. Similarly, Jonathan Holden has spoken of the importance of syntax

in the poetry: "It is Ashbery's genius . . . to perceive that syntax in writing is the equivalent of 'composition' in painting: it has an intrinsic beauty and authority almost wholly independent of any specific context" ("Syntax and the Poetry of John Ashbery," *American Poetry Review* 8.4 [July/August 1979], 37).

19. John Vernon, "Fresh Air: Humor in Contemporary American Poetry," in Sarah Blacher Cohen, ed., *Comic Relief: Humor in Contemporary American Literature* (Urbana: University of Illinois Press, 1978), 305.

20. Stitt, 46–47.

21. Stitt, 57. Ashbery went on to explain here: "When I was fresh out of college, Abstract Expressionism was the most exciting thing in the arts. There was also experimental music and film, but poetry seemed quite conventional in comparison. I guess it still is, in a way. One can accept a Picasso woman with two noses, but an equivalent attempt in poetry baffles the same audience."

22. Poulin, 251–52. Just as he has drawn on painting for models of some of his techniques, Ashbery has also expressed an interest in the ways of music: "What I like about music is its ability of being convincing, of carrying an argument through successfully to the finish, though the terms of this argument remain unknown quantities. What remains is the structure, the architecture of the argument, scene or story. I would like to do this in poetry" (from Ashbery's brief statement in the "Biographies and Bibliography" section of *A Controversy of Poets: An Anthology of Contemporary American Poetry*, ed. Paris Leary and Robert Kelly [New York: Doubleday, 1965], 523).

23. Stitt, 35.

24. Just how plugged into reality Ashbery is may be judged from the answer he gave when an interviewer asked him: "What are you doing when you're writing poetry that you wouldn't be doing if you were, say, writing an essay?" Ashbery answered: "I like the situation of trying to communicate something to somebody even in the crudest forms of yellow journalism. I get carried away and start to cry when I read some article in a tabloid newspaper about a woman who accidentally flushed her baby down the toilet or something like that. This seems like real life" (John Koethe, "An Interview with John Ashbery," *SubStance* 37/38 [1983], 180).

25. Stitt, 54–55.

26. Shapiro, 23–24.

27. "Craft Interview with John Ashbery," *New York Quarterly* 9 (1972), 21–22.

STEPHEN DOBYNS

1. Rosalind E. Krauss, *Passages in Modern Sculpture* (New York: Viking Press, 1977), 3.
2. Robert Hellenga, *The Sixteen Pleasures* (New York: Delta, 1994), 148–49.
3. *Concurring Beasts* is the title of Dobyns' first book, which was published as the Lamont Poetry Selection in 1971. "Passing the Word" appears near the end of that volume; by placing it first in his selected volume, Dobyns is choosing to give it much greater importance. Of the forty-three poems in the original volume, only fourteen are reprinted in the selected volume; the ratio is higher for later books.
4. Gilbert Allen, "Cool, Calm & Collected," *American Book Review* 6.4 (May-June 1984), 20.
5. Dobyns did not reprint his prefatory note with the poems he selected from *The Balthus Poems* for reprinting in *Velocities*; thus I quote from the earlier volume.
6. The first of the negative comments is from an anonymous review of *Concurring Beasts* that appeared in *Antioch Review* 32 (1972), 242; the second is from Robert D. Spector's review of the same book that appeared in *Saturday Review* (11 March 1972), 80. The positive view is from Ron Slate's "Thick with Discovery," *Chowder Review* 8 (1977), 56.
7. Robert Hass described the process followed in *The Balthus Poems* by contrasting it to what happens in Dobyns' crime novels: "The detective in the poems is [the poet's] own imagination. As it enters this world, it colludes with it. Detective and criminal become one, and the criminal is the heart, or rather it is the heart as it begins to understand the body's fate" (review of *The Balthus Poems*, *Book World — The Washington Post* [5 September 1982], 7).
8. Dobyns' narrative method, in this poem in particular, but elsewhere as well, resembles that of Louis Simpson, who in recent years has been writing brilliant narrative poems characterized by a prosaic style that draws its characters, images, and events from everyday life. Specifically, the situation in Dobyns' "How to Like It" resembles that in Simpson's "Quiet Desperation," which features a middle-aged man who struggles against his sense of worthlessness and fear of death while he is out walking the family dog. One of Dobyns' lines ("the desire to get in a car and just keep driving") also resembles a question in Simpson's poem "Dinner at the Sea-View Inn": "Wouldn't it be great to hire a taxi / and just keep going?" When I asked Dobyns about these parallels between his work and Simpson's, however, he emphatically denied any influence, adding that he has hardly even read Simpson's poems. For a fuller discussion of "Quiet Des-

peration" and other Simpson poems, see the essay in my earlier book *The World's Hieroglyphic Beauty.*

9. Peter Cooley, review of *Concurring Beasts, North American Review* 258.1 (Spring 1973), 72.

10. Richard Jackson, "No Language but the Language of the Heart," *Prairie Schooner* 56 (1982), 97.

11. Mary Kinzie, "How Could Fools Get Tired!" *Poetry* 132.1 (April 1978), 45.

CHARLES SIMIC

1. Steven Cramer, "Goddesses, Gods, and Devils," *Poetry* 159.4 (January 1992), 228.

2. "The Light Is Dark Enough," *Hudson Review* 34.1 (1981), 150. Despite the excellence of Young's insight, and scattered good comments by other critics elsewhere, it is hard not to feel that Simic's readers in general have not quite been up to the challenge of his work. The two best essays on him — neither of which is to the point of the present essay — are by Peter Schmidt (*"White:* Charles Simic's Thumbnail Epic," *Contemporary Literature* 23 [1982], 528–49) and Kevin Hart ("Writing Things: Literary Property in Heidegger and Simic," *New Literary History,* 21 [1989], 199–214).

3. Charles Simic, "With Sherod Santos," *The Uncertain Certainty* (Ann Arbor: University of Michigan Press, 1992), 68.

4. Charles Simic, "Wonderful Words, Silent Truth," in *Wonderful Words, Silent Truth: Essays on Poetry and A Memoir* (Ann Arbor: University of Michigan Press, 1990), 87.

5. Simic, "Reading Philosophy at Night," *Wonderful Words, Silent Truth,* 58.

6. Helen Vendler, "Totemic Sifting," *Parnassus: Poetry in Review* 18.2 & 19.1 (combined issue, 1993), 99.

7. Simic, *Wonderful Words, Silent Truth,* 94.

8. The conversation took place on the *McNeil/Lehrer News Hour* on PBS, December 29, 1993.

9. Review of *Weather Forecast for Utopia and Vicinity: Poems 1967–1982, Publishers Weekly* 224.18 (28 October 1983), 67–68.

10. Interview with Rick Jackson and Michael Panori, in *The Uncertain Certainty,* 62–63.

11. Matthew Flamm, "Impersonal Best: Charles Simic Loses Himself," *Virginia Quarterly Review* 51 (December 1986), 18.

12. Simic, "Notes on Poetry and Philosophy," *Wonderful Words, Silent Truth,* 63.

13. Simic, "Wonderful Words, Silent Truth," 90.

14. Simic, *Wonderful Words, Silent Truth*, 60–61. Elsewhere Simic has given this more prosaic definition: "I think in the twentieth century humor has become ontological. It's a permanent disruption, it's a world view, a philosophy of life. Everything is equally tragic and comic . . ." (interview "With Wayne Dodd and Stanley Plumly," *The Uncertain Certainty*, 19).

15. Simic, "Notes on Poetry and History," *The Uncertain Certainty*, 127.

16. Interview with Rick Jackson and Michael Panori, in *The Uncertain Certainty*, 59.

17. Geoffrey Thurley, "Devices among Words: Kinnell, Bly, Simic," in his *The American Moment: American Poetry in the Mid-Century* (New York: St. Martin's Press, 1978), 226.

18. Vendler, 97–98.

19. Vendler, 87.

20. Simic, "Wonderful Words, Silent Truth," 92. Simic's most recent statement on his religious feelings is contained in an essay scheduled to be published in a symposium on poetry and religion in *New Letters*; I quote from the very end of Simic's manuscript: "'Every poem, knowingly or unknowingly, is addressed to God,' the poet Frank Samperi told me long ago. I remember . . . objecting. . . . No more. Today I think as he did then. It makes absolutely no difference whether gods and devils exist or not. The secret ambition of every true poem is to ask about them even as it acknowledges their absence."

21. "Wonderful Words, Silent Truth," 88.

22. "Wonderful Words, Silent Truth," 89.

23. "Notes on Poetry and Philosophy," 66–67.

24. "Notes on Poetry and Philosophy," 67.

25. Simic, "Negative Capability and Its Children," *The Uncertain Certainty*, 91.

26. Vendler, 91.

27. Vendler, 92.

28. "Wonderful Words, Silent Truth," 88.

29. Vendler, 94.

30. "Wonderful Words, Silent Truth," 90.

31. Robert Atwan, review of *Unending Blues*, *Los Angeles Times Book Review* (7 December 1986), 8.

32. Michael Milburn, "Fresh Forks & Original Vision," *New Letters Review of Books* I.1 (Spring 1987), 10; Flamm, 18.

33. Edward Larrissy, "Home and Abroad," *Poetry Review* 73.2 (June 1983), 65; David Dooley, review of *Selected Poems*, *Hudson Review* 44.1 (Spring 1991), 158–59.

34. "Wonderful Words, Silent Truth," 92. Critic Robert B. Shaw noticed the in-

creased expression of affection in Simic's poems as early as the volume *Return to a Place Lit by a Glass of Milk*: "Human beings had rarely appeared as major subjects in *Dismantling the Silence*. Now Simic has come to admit them more often to his view of the world, including in the contents of *Return*, a poem about his father and some remarkable love poems" ("Charles Simic: An Appreciation," *New Republic* [24 January 1976], 26).

35. Simic, "In the Beginning . . . ," *Wonderful Words, Silent Truth*, 10–11.

36. "In the Beginning . . . ," 53.

GERALD STERN

1. As Steven Cramer has observed, the typical Stern poem consists of "syntactical catalogues . . . running anywhere from nine lines to three pages, [that] interweave explicit or implicit narrative. . . . the best of these poems sound the historical resonances of individual sorrow or joy" ("Four True Voices of Feeling," *Poetry* 157.2 [November 1990], 111).

2. Frederick Garber, "Pockets of Secrecy, Places of Occasion: On Gerald Stern," *American Poetry Review* 15.4 (July/August 1986), 41.

3. Garber, 43. In addressing the same subject, Jane Somerville characterizes Stern's voice correctly while seeming not to recognize Whitman's similarly rich sense of humor: "But Whitman's character is played straight, while Stern's is not. The Stern speaker is comic as well as grand; his heroics are undermined by irreverence, irony, and jestful self-mockery" (*Making the Light Come: The Poetry of Gerald Stern* [Detroit: Wayne State University Press, 1990], 14).

4. The essay is reprinted in *Collected Prose* by James Wright, edited by Anne Wright (Ann Arbor: University of Michigan Press, 1983), 3–22.

5. Somerville, 56.

6. The class was held on April 19, 1994.

7. David Wojahn, review of *The Red Coal*, *Poetry East* 6 (Fall 1981), 96–97.

8. Surprisingly, the poet and critic Edward Hirsch, overlooking Stern's use of metaphor, thought that this poem was based not on the recognition that the bodies of some Jews were used to make soap by the Nazis, but on the "odd, semihumorous . . . finding [of] small bars of soap in human shape" ("A Late, Ironic Whitman," *Nation* 240.2 [19 January 1985], 56).

9. How nonoccasional the persecution of the Jews has been is illustrated by a story that Stern tells about his youth in Pittsburgh, when he felt he was "the victim of anti-Semitic slurs and physical abuse all during my early childhood — until we moved into a Jewish neighborhood when I was ten" ("Some

Secrets," in *In Praise of What Persists*, ed. Stephen Berg [New York: Harper & Row, 1983], 258).

10. David Wojahn takes a somewhat more negative view of Stern's use of form than I do: "Though Stern is often a poignant phrasemaker, and makes dazzling use of metaphor, his power comes more from the abundance of his spirit than it does from his command of technique. He cares little for prosody, and his long Whitmanesque lines, more-or-less iambic, often grow redundant. Since his concerns are so obsessive, his method can seem obsessive, too. The poems show too much similarity in their development, almost always following the same rhetorical framework" (review of *The Red Coal*, 101–102).

11. Of all Stern's critics, Jane Somerville has best expressed his use of consciousness to unify and transform the world of reality: "He transforms himself endlessly, playing whatever parts appeal to him, yet his identity never changes: whether he takes the mask of a friendly gardener, a wandering hero, a rabbinical figure, a fallen angel, a god—even a tree or bird—he is still the same whimsical guy, a fantastic prophet and favorite uncle who, though full of wisdom, permits himself all manner of weakness, readily admits to his own foolishness, indulges in spates of sentiment, suffers endlessly, and overcomes suffering through imagination. In the gap between his vast proportions and his foolishness we recognize the human condition; in his capacity for transformation he becomes a metaphor for imagination" (Somerville, 12).

12. During an interview with Mark Hillringhouse, Stern discussed his heavy use of one of these devices: "My use of repetition—Anaphora, it's called—comes partly from Whitman, partly from the Bible. We're referring to the same word or words being repeated at the beginning of succeeding lines, or verses, right? It's an ancient system. Like rhyme, and English stress, and free verse, it lends itself to misuse. It's something that just took me over—I didn't adopt it. I don't know why" (Mark Hillringhouse, "Gerald Stern: An Interview," *American Poetry Review* 13.2 [March/April 1984], 30). Critics have of course been attentive to this musical aspect of Stern's work, Somerville going so far as to say that Stern's "verbal audacity is surprising, especially when compared with the safe, dull humming that characterizes so much of today's poetry" (Somerville, 14). Far more surprising, perhaps, is the deafness exhibited by Emily Grosholz, who argues that the "failure of narrative import" in Stern's work "is echoed at the level of form: brief, irregular lines in brief, irregular stanzas linked by the flat repetition of words or phrases. Josephine Miles has observed that contemporary American poets do not fully exploit the formal resources of repetition

in their poetry. In general, they restrict themselves to alliteration, forgetting that repetition at the level of word, phrase, and sentence provides the extra dimension of semantic as well as aural resonance, where each new instance may be subtle amplification, or ironic undermining, of the original" ("Family Ties," *Hudson Review* 37 [1985], 653). Of course Stern does all these things, and in precisely the manner described by the uncomprehending critic.

CHARLES WRIGHT

1. Harold B. Segal, *The Baroque Poem: A Comparative Survey* (New York: E. P. Dutton, 1974), 104.
2. Segal, 30.
3. Lowell's review was published on the front page of the *New York Times Book Review* for March 21, 1971. The changes in Kunitz' style have naturally provoked a good bit of comment from other critics, who do not always agree about the value, nor even about the meaning, of the changes. For example, Marjorie Perloff, whose interest in poetry is centered almost entirely in the area of content, indicated in writing of *The Testing Tree* her dislike for "the clever but ultimately empty verbalism that detracted from his early poems"; she went on to hope that the "66-year-old Kunitz has finally found a lyric mode that suits his native temperament" ("The Testing of Stanley Kunitz," *Iowa Review* 3 [1972], 98, 93–94). Gregory Orr seems to like the styles equally well, but sees the change as in matters much more profound than mere verbal surfaces: "There *is* a stylistic shift, but more deeply than that there is a fundamental shift in Kunitz's relation to the world and to his life. If the earlier poems were often structured as intense, lyricized metaphysical and intellectual allegories whose discoveries and dramas involved transcending the physical world, then the later work is marked by a deep shift toward acceptance of the physical world and the existence of others. The intensity of many early Kunitz poems is the intensity of passionate intellect, but later work opens itself to a new world of feeling" (*American Poetry Review* 9.4 [July/August 1980], 36). In my interview with him, Kunitz himself commented on the significance of the alteration in his style, emphasizing the notion of continuity over that of radical change: "Some years ago, in commenting on my later work, I said I was trying to write poems with a surface so simple and transparent that you could look through them and see the world. I didn't mean to suggest that I had lost interest in the orchestration of the world within. Texture is more than a superficial phenomenon and is not to be confused with the maintenance of a high style. My main concern is

with psychic texture, which is a deeper and more complex thing" (Peter Stitt, "An Interview with Stanley Kunitz," *Gettysburg Review* 5 [1992], 207).

4. Stanley Kunitz, *A Kind of Order, a Kind of Folly: Essays and Conversations* (Boston: Little, Brown, 1975), 310.

5. Daniel Halpern, "Things That Make the World Worth Saving: An Introduction to a Poetry Reading," in *A Celebration for Stanley Kunitz on His Eightieth Birthday* (Riverdale-on-Hudson: Sheep Meadow Press, 1986), 129.

6. Although some critics see Kunitz' early poems as relatively impersonal (see the comment of Gregory Orr in note 3 above), most agree with my perception of them as deeply emotional. David Ignatow, for example, speaks of his amazement at "how one man could contain such pressing and powerful emotions within traditional forms that had certainly been invented with the purpose of supporting and illustrating in themselves an elegant accommodation to life" ("A Figure of Change and Freedom," *Antaeus* 37 [1980], 129). Ralph J. Mills, Jr., commenting on Kunitz' early "Hermetic Poem," similarly says: "Poetic language under the conditions implied by this poem is stretched to the snapping point by the surge of emotions pressing against it. What Jean Hagstrum speaks of as Kunitz' 'imagistic surrealism' accurately describes this phenomenon" (*Contemporary American Poetry* [New York: Random House, 1965], 40; Hagstrum's pioneering study of Kunitz' early poems, "The Poetry of Stanley Kunitz: An Introductory Essay," appears in *Poets in Progress*, ed. Edward Hungerford [Evanston: Northwestern University Press, 1967]).

7. Kunitz, *A Kind of Order*, 126.

8. Gregory Orr has also noticed this characteristic of Kunitz' early poems, though he puts a more portentous spin on it than I do: "At this stage, Kunitz sees poetry as a noble, occult calling; one in which the high mysteries of art, metaphysics, and religion may reveal themselves to the man who steeps himself in secret, sacred knowledge" (*Stanley Kunitz: An Introduction to the Poetry* [New York: Columbia University Press, 1985], 49).

9. Many critics have noticed Kunitz' debt to the British metaphysical poets, but Michael Ryan has expressed it best: "Because of Eliot's essays, a great enthusiasm for metaphysical poetry filled the air in the twenties and thirties, so much so that literary historians refer to it as the Metaphysical Revival. What the Modern temperament, and I believe Kunitz, admired in that poetry is its intensity . . . , its 'wit' . . . , and its [in Eliot's words] 'direct sensuous apprehension of thought, or recreation of thought into feeling'" ("The Early Poems: Isolation and Apocalypse," *Antaeus* 37 [1980], 142).

10. Kunitz' commitment to self-expression, even in his seemingly more objective early poems, has been noticed by other critics. Marie Henault, for example, said this of "Vita Nuova": "It is a fierce, solemn poem of self-examination and revelation, typically introspective and hard on the self in its asserting a new determination to be dedicated to a singleness one rarely achieves" (*American Poets, 1880–1945*, vol. 48 of *Dictionary of Literary Biography*, second series [Detroit: Gale Research, 1986], 269). Similarly, Robert Weisberg points out that Kunitz "manages to bring to his immediate experience a Renaissance sense of wit and decorum, including metrical formality, and use it to express and contain his personality, not suppress it through derivative stylization" ("Stanley Kunitz: The Stubborn Middle Way," *Modern Poetry Studies* 6 [1975], 54).

11. Stanley Kunitz, "On 'Father and Son,' " in *The Contemporary Poet as Artist and Critic*, ed. Anthony Ostroff (Boston: Little, Brown, 1964), 78.

12. Segal, 29, 30.

13. J. D. McClatchy, "The Art of Poetry XLI: Charles Wright," *Paris Review* 113 (1989), 201.

14. Review of *Bloodlines*, *New York Times Book Review* (7 September 1975), 14.

15. Charles Wright, *Halflife: Improvisations and Interviews, 1977–87* (Ann Arbor: University of Michigan Press, 1988), 138.

16. Charles Wright, *Contemporary Authors: Autobiography Series*, vol. 7, ed. Mark Zadrozny (Detroit: Gale Research, 1989), 291.

17. Two other critics have written about this poem, both of them largely in agreement with my perspective. Carol Muske sees the poem as "an object lesson, substantiating itself with the shapes of the developing calligraphy, abstraction made sensuous and morphous before our eyes" ("Ourselves as History," *Parnassus: Poetry in Review* 4.2 [1976], 117), while Kathleen Agena says: "the whole poem is about words, about the way they come to carry meaning, the dynamic that exists between words as signifiers and the things they signify, the guilt of words as opposed to the purity of silence" ("The Mad Sense of Language," *Partisan Review* 43 [1976], 627).

18. Wright, *Contemporary Authors*, 292.

19. Other critics have written on the role of religion in Wright's work. Helen Vendler, for example, contrasts Wright's strong sense of doubt with Montale's troubled certainty: "The spiritual yearning in Wright is nowhere rewarded, as it sometimes is in Montale, by a certain faith in an absolute — damaged no doubt, elusive surely, disagreeable often, but always unquestioned and recoverable" (*Part of Nature, Part of Us* [Cambridge: Harvard University Press, 1980], 287). George F. Butterick comes to a similar conclusion: "Each time

[Wright] returns to this theme, his faith in nature is unshaken and, if anything, stronger than ever, while religion continues to appear extraneous" ("Charles Wright," *Dictionary of Literary Biography Yearbook: 1982* [Detroit: Gale Research, 1982], 399).

20. Segal, 116.
21. Wright, *Halflife*, 153, 154.
22. Wright, *Contemporary Authors*, 293, 296.
23. Wright, *Halflife*, 184.
24. Speaking of the many ghosts that people Wright's poems, George F. Butterick has said: "As [can] be seen throughout his work, there are presences in his imagination that the material world alone cannot explain" ("Charles Wright," 391). Calvin Bedient, in his radically disconnective and almost unreadable review of *The Southern Cross*, suggests that pursuing the dead is the sum of Wright's thematic quest in all his work: "Not that Wright is occult: on the contrary, he would make the intangible stark. To him revelation came early and has remained unsparing: it is that the dead, who are superior to us, who know more and feel more, are always near us. He hails the superhuman, writes of death-in-life and life-in-death" ("Tracing Charles Wright," *Parnassus: Poetry in Review* 10.1 [1982], 55).
25. McClatchy, 192.
26. As Floyd Collins wrote in his review of *The World of the Ten Thousand Things*, after reading an earlier version of the present essay: "Wright's self-portraitures in *The Other Side of the River* increasingly depict incident and anecdote within the context of place — the present belonging to California, the past to Italy and the American South, the future to that mysterious river with one shore in the temporal world, the other in eternity" ("Metamorphosis within the Poetry of Charles Wright," *Gettysburg Review* 4 [1991], 470).
27. Bruce Bond, "Metaphysics of the Image in Charles Wright and Paul Cézanne," *Southern Review* 30.1 (1994), 116.
28. Vendler, *Part of Nature, Part of Us*, 287.
29. Mary Kinzie sees places as crucial in Wright's poems and also sees them at times as leading to the otherworldly: "Wright could be said to depend absolutely on place, to work from it, in his crucial journeys, traced in so many poems, from rest to intense engagement with ethereal thresholds, tints of light, floating gestures" ("Haunting," *American Poetry Review* 11.5 [September/October 1982], 40). Rather than seeing this progression as embodying Wright's peculiar strength as I do, however, Kinzie — who doesn't like Wright's poems — prefers to see it as another sign of his love simply for that which is

insubstantial. Robert Pinsky takes a position close to mine when he points out how Wright links the concrete and the abstract, often through setting: "Repeatedly, Wright finds his most compelling voice when the described locale and the foliating poetic language are balanced by their relation to some moral abstraction — often an abstraction simultaneously hollow and powerful, like 'Salvation' in . . . lines about a childhood Bible camp" ("Description and the Virtuous Use of Words," *Parnassus: Poetry in Review* 3.2 [1975], 145).

30. Charles Wright, "Improvisations: Narrative of the Image (A Correspondence with Charles Simic)," *Gettysburg Review* 8.1 (1995), 9–21.

31. This way of handling death has been noticed as well by Helen Vendler: "To Wright, death is as often ascent as burial; we become stars, like Romeo, after death, as often as roses" (*Part of Nature, Part of Us*, 286).

32. Samuel Johnson, "Life of Cowley," in his *Lives of the Poets*.

33. Pinsky, 143.

34. X. J. Kennedy, "A Tenth and Four Fifths," *Poetry* 141 (March 1983), 357.

35. Kinzie, 40.

36. Bedient, "Slide-Wheeling around the Curves," *Southern Review* 27.1 (Winter 1991), 230, 221.

37. Richard Jackson, "Worlds Created, Worlds Perceived," *Michigan Quarterly Review* 17 (1978), 556. Kathleen Agena similarly noticed the commitment to language as subject in Wright's early work: "all three of his [early] books contain poems which, strictly speaking, refer only to words and their maneuverings" (626).

38. McClatchy, 204–205.

39. For a fuller discussion of this aspect of Robert Penn Warren's work, see my chapter on him in *The World's Hieroglyphic Beauty: Five American Poets* (Athens: University of Georgia Press, 1985).

40. McClatchy, 205.

Index